Christmas Puzzles

Publications International, Ltd.

Puzzle creators: Cihan Altay, Helem An, Chris Bolton, Keith Burns, Myles Callum, Philip Carter, Mark Danna, Harvey Estes, Josie Faulkner, Marilynn Huret, Steve Karp, Naomi Lipsky, Dan Meinking, Michael Moreci, Fred Piscop, Ratselmeister, Dave Roberts, Marilyn Roberts, Stephen Ryder, Gianni Sarcone, Pete Sarjeant, Paul Seaburn, Terry Stickels, Nicole Sulgit, Jen Torche, Wayne Robert Williams

Puzzle illustrators: Helem An, Elizabeth Gerber, Pat Hagle, Robin Humer, Shavan R. Spears, Jen Torche

Louis Weber, CEO
Publications International, Ltd.
8140 Lehigh Avenue
Morton Grove, IL 60053

ISBN: 978-1-68022-643-0

Manufactured in China.

8 7 6 5 4 3 2 1

'TIS THE SEASON TO BE PUZZLING

The holidays approach, schedules fill up, the anticipation grows—and so does the need to sit down and recharge with some Christmas puzzles! The fun puzzles inside will leave you refreshed and ready to get right back to the shopping, wrapping, baking, and socializing— whatever is on your December calendar. We've packed this book with lots of different kinds of puzzles, and they all have Christmas themes. From word ladders and scrambled sentences to anagrams and visual puzzles, there's something for every kind of puzzler.

These puzzles are great for de-stressing, but they also stimulate your brain in important ways. Research shows that even a relatively brief regimen of vigorous cognitive activity often produces perceptible and lasting effects. As with physical exercise, the results are best when cognitive exercise becomes a regular habit. So consider keeping the puzzles handy in a backpack or purse. You'll be giving your brain a great workout—and staying in the holiday spirit too.

White Christmas

Every word listed below is contained within the group of letters. Words can be found in a straight line horizontally, vertically, or diagonally. They may read either forward or backward. When complete, the leftover letters will spell out a Christmas quote from E. B. White.

BLITZEN	MERRY
CANDY	MRS. CLAUS
CHIMNEY	PRANCER
COMET	RIBBONS
CUPID	ROOFTOP
DANCER	RUDOLPH
DASHER	ST. NICK
DONNER	STOCKINGS
ELVES	TOYS
GIFTS	VIXEN
JOLLY	YULETIDE

HIDDEN QUOTE:

_____

```
T O D P E R D S C E I V R H E
C H A R I O S G S E V L E P T
M A N S N T H N I R O U C L G
H Y C N T N I I T F S W N O R
A M E P P E I K N G T B A D C
E R R N C Z M C J O M S R U S
E E S S M T R O O F T O P R T
M H M O C I L T C R V I X E N
E S E A S L H S D I D F F I I
R A N C Y B A C U L T W I T C
R D H E O V E U R Y Y E A R K
Y U L E T I D E S N O B B I R
```

Twisted Path

Starting from the X, draw a continuous path that twists around all the trees once without the path crossing itself, though it may continue adjacent to itself. The path should be as short as possible and cannot go between 2 black dots. The path should lead you back to the X.

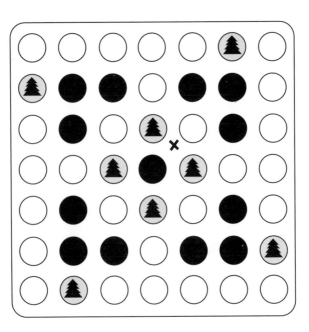

Wacky Wordy

Can you "read" a word from the letters below?

ABCDEFGHIJKMNOPQRSTUVWXYZ

Picture This

Place each of the 15 boxes in the 3 by 5 grid below so that they form a holiday picture. Do this without cutting the page apart.

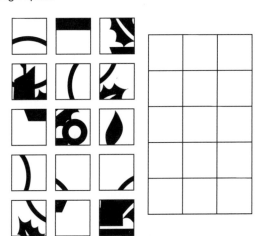

Answers on page 166.

Word Ladder

Use the clues to change just one letter on each line to go from the top word to the bottom word. Do not change the order of the letters. You must have a common English word at each step.

YULE

_____ donkey crossbreed

_____ no sound

_____ stringed instrument

_____ light toboggan

_____ hauls

LOGS

Anagram

Unscramble the words below to create words or terms related to Christmas. When complete, the first letter of each new word or phrase will combine to spell another wintry word.

1. CASUAL ANTS: 2 wds.

2. HELP OR NOT: 2 wds.

3. SENT ROMAN: 1 wd.

4. WIN SEEM: 2 wds.

Holiday Cheer

Every word listed is contained within the 2 letter grids. Words wrap up, down, and side to side. One word has already been found for you.

Grid 1:

S	R	E	T	W	F	L	A	P	O
T	W	I	N	O	N	S	K	H	L
H	G	I	L	S	A	M	E	T	E
S	S	S	T	F	I	T	S	R	O
T	E	B	E	C	G	S	R	E	N
N	L	A	M	E	C	I	G	E	S
E	B	U	B	D	H	R	R	T	D
M	S	R	E	S	A	N	E	I	R
A	U	A	L	C	A	T	I	N	A
N	R	O	R	E	E	D	N	G	C

Word list (right of grid 1):

BAUBLES
CANDY CANE
CAROLS
CHRISTMAS LIGHTS
CHRISTMAS TREE
DECEMBER
ELVES
GIFTS
GINGERBREAD
GREETING CARDS
HOLLY

Word list (left of grid 2):

MISTLETOE
NORTH POLE
NUTCRACKER
ORNAMENTS
POINSETTIA
REINDEER
ROBIN
SANTA CLAUS
SNOWFLAKES
SNOWMAN
TOY FACTORY
WINTER

Grid 2:

E	R	O	W	M	A	N	R	B	R
K	S	N	T	S	I	M	E	G	E
C	A	R	L	E	T	O	E	N	A
H	C	C	T	U	N	S	S	I	D
R	S	E	T	T	I	E	L	G	E
I	N	I	O	P	A	V	O	C	N
S	T	M	A	S	E	L	R	A	A
T	E	E	R	T	Y	C	A	N	C
O	A	C	T	O	R	N	I	D	Y
Y	F	Y	L	L	O	H	B	O	R

Christmas Tamagram

Find an expression to define the picture below, and then rearrange the letters of it to form a 9-letter word. LLL, for example, is THREE L'S, which transforms to SHELTER.

Too Many Santas

How many times can you read SANTA in the grid by proceeding from letter to consecutive letter horizontally, vertically, and diagonally?

S	A	N	T	S
N	A	T	A	A
T	N	S	N	T
A	A	T	A	N
S	T	N	A	S

Answers on page 167.

Happy Christmas

The letters in SNOW can be found in boxes 6, 7, 12, and 16, but not necessarily in that order. Similarly, the letters in all the other words can be found in the boxes indicated. Your task is to insert all the letters of the alphabet into the boxes. If you do this correctly, the shaded cells will reveal another word associated with Christmas.

1	2	3	4	5	6	7	8	9	10	11	12	13

14	15	16	17	18	19	20	21	22	23	24	25	26

ADVENT: 4, 6, 8, 13, 14, 20

BAUBLES: 7, 8, 9, 11, 18, 20

BLAZING FIRE: 1, 5, 6, 8, 9, 11, 17, 20, 25, 26

CHOCOLATE: 2, 4, 8, 9, 12, 20, 24

CRACKERS: 7, 8, 20, 22, 24, 26

FAIRY: 3, 5, 20, 25, 26

HOLLY: 2, 3, 9, 12

JINGLE BELLS: 1, 5, 6, 7, 8, 9, 11, 21

LIQUEURS: 5, 7, 8, 9, 18, 23, 26

MISTLETOE: 4, 5, 7, 8, 9, 12, 19

PRESENTS: 4, 6, 7, 8, 10, 26

REINDEER: 5, 6, 8, 13, 26

SNOW: 6, 7, 12, 16

XMAS LIGHTS: 1, 2, 4, 5, 7, 9, 15, 19, 20

YULE LOG: 1, 3, 8, 9, 12, 18

The Heart of Christmas

Every word or phrase listed below is contained within the grid of letters. Words can be found in a straight line horizontally, vertically, or diagonally. They may read either forward or backward. When complete, the leftover letters spell out a Christmas quote from Roy L. Smith.

ANGELS

BETHLEHEM

CARDS

CAROLS

CHIMNEY

CUPID

DECK THE HALLS

DONNER

FROSTY

GIFTS

HOLLY

ICICLE

JOLLY

MAGI

MANGER

MERRY

MYRRH

NOEL

PUNCH

REINDEER

SILENT NIGHT

SLEIGH BELLS

SNOWMAN

STAR

ST. NICK

TIDINGS

TINSEL

TOYS

TURKEY

VIXEN

WINTER

WRAPPING

PAPER

WREATH

HIDDEN QUOTE:

_____

```
H E W D R N H O H S M A Y S N
O T S L E I G H B E L L S C H
R I T X P C S T R T L O D H S
M A I S A I K R N O E L R T I
H V D N P C Y T J Y E H A A I
M C I S G L H H H S T R C E C
E A N E N E C G N E C S R R A
H H G U I U R I T W H E O W G
E O S I P D T N I W I A S R I
L L L I P L O T I N M R L N F
H L D E A V E N D R N E E L T
T Y E K R U T E N F E G G I S
E N D I W E E L T E Y N N U N
B D M Y R R H I E R R A A A T
R E K C I N T S N O W M A N E
```

Word Columns

Find the hidden quote from Bill Watterson by using the letters directly below each of the blank squares. Each letter is used once. A black square indicates the end of a word.

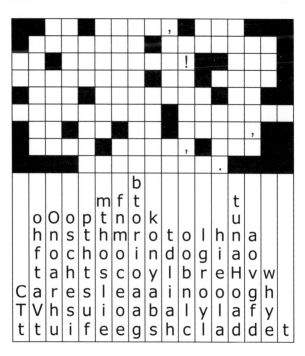

Say What?

Below is a group of words that, when properly arranged in the blanks, reveals a quote from Victor Borge.

idea the people year once right

Santa Claus has _____ _____ _____. Visit _____
_____ a _____.

One Time

Find the word "elf" once—and only once—in the word grid below.

```
F E L L F F E
E L E F E F L
L E F L L F E
L F L F E F E
F L F E F E L
E F E L F L L
L E F E L E F
```

Word Ladder

Change just one letter on each line to go from the top word to the bottom word. Do not change the order of the letters. You must have a common English word at each step.

REIN

_____ carries blood

_____ worn by a bride

_____

_____ pass out cards

_____

DEER

St. Nick's Sidekicks

Cryptograms are messages in substitution code. Break the code to read the message. For example, THE SMART CAT might become FVO QWGDF JGF if F is substituted for T, V for H, O for E, and so on.

CBDNB VGBWC PBC CLFS VLGLOAWG VLFUBDYLDC YD

SWOLUSBD VLWDNOYSC. NPSQ YDVGWES NPS GYFUYDZ,

CLLN-VLMSOSE XDSVPN OWUOSVPN; NPS AOSDVP UÈOS

ALWSNNBOE, B CYDYCNSO VPBOBVNSO JPL VBOOYSC JPYUC;

NPS CVBOQ-GLLXYDZ XOBFUWC LA BWCNOYB BDE DSBOIQ

VLWDNOYSC; BDE NPS AWO-JSBOYDZ ISGCDYVXSG LA

ZSOFBDQ BDE USDDCQGMBDYB EWNVP VLWDNOQC, JPL FBQ

GSBMS B GWFU LA VLBG YD NPS CNLVXYDZC LA DBWZPNQ

VPYGEOSD!

Snowed-Men

Find the one thing in common in each of the 8 rows of snowmen (horizontally, vertically, and diagonally).

Hiding Some Christmas Things

ACROSS
1. Kismet
5. Army chow
9. Plays and such
14. Norwegian king
15. Southernmost Great Lake
16. External
17. Tennis ace Sampras
18. Clay deposit
19. Hot ___ buns
20. Christmas character disguised as a jazz guitarist?
23. "An Inconvenient Truth" narrator
24. Big web portal
25. Wine from Jerez
28. It dissolved in 1991: abbr.
30. "Pow!"
33. Went sniggling
34. On the ocean
35. Some arias
36. Christmas plant hiding in a showbiz TV show?
39. Make more watery
40. "Don't Hassel the _____": "Baywatch" star motto
41. Curses
42. Twenty-volume dictionary: abbr.
43. Informal greeting
44. Big-brimmed bonnet
45. Flattens, for short
46. Kind of music
47. Christmas song hiding in a southeastern state?
53. Portuguese enclave in China
54. "It's beginning to look _____ like..."
55. Smooth sailing
57. Hawke of "Dead Poets Society"
58. Ritzy
59. Tizzy
60. "A Confederacy of Dunces" author
61. Head of France?
62. Garden hopper

DOWN
1. Dandy
2. A Baldwin
3. Soho sign-off
4. Christmas tree type
5. Down _____ lane
6. Obliterate
7. Galahad and others

Answers on page 168.

8. Actress Ward
9. Advanced degree holder
10. Cracker-barrel
11. Gobs
12. Western elevation
13. Word in the MGM motto
21. Byron and Tennyson
22. Typical French vowel
25. Defense group abolished in 1977: abbr.
26. Anne of "Men in Trees"
27. Spanish hero of yore
28. "The good ol' _____"
29. Egotist's obsession
30. Diner seat
31. Hilo hello
32. Central part

34. Mate's shout
35. Most elegant
37. "Skewer" in Istanbul
38. "Try it, _____ like it!"
43. Knee-slapper
44. Comfort
45. African cattle pen
46. On the windowpane
47. Kosovo force
48. Eight in Ecuador
49. Above 1st Lt.: abbr.
50. Soothing botanical
51. Prefix with second
52. Where Bhutan is
53. Bumped into
56. Airport abbr.

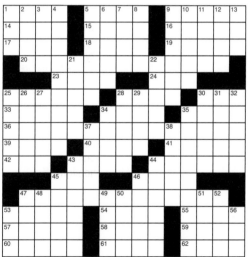

Red and Green

ACROSS
1. Culinary concoction
5. Bubbly drink
9. Viewpoint
14. Sudden inspiration
15. Big birds Down Under
16. Poops out
17. Santa's ride
19. Root veggies
20. Earmark
21. Make a decision
22. Walk to and fro
23. Heavy hammer
25. Feigns
29. Humanitarian organization
31. Beat walker
32. Burns wildly
35. Come to a stop
36. Sensible
37. Miscalculates
38. Seethes
39. Small, brown bird
40. Stage signals
41. More than that
42. Took on, as cargo
43. Bart Simpson's grandpa
44. Packers' home
46. Carolina team
48. Solution
52. Tango teams
53. Tax-deferred letters
54. Chopping tool
55. Buenos _____, Argentina
57. Stop commands
60. Type of target shooting
61. Burn balm
62. Yesteryear
63. Mary-Louise Parker Showtime hit
64. Skillfully deceptive
65. Castle ringer

DOWN
1. Loam, loess, etc.
2. Absolutely perfect
3. Marsh grass
4. Possesses
5. Oozed
6. Fail to include
7. Used shovels
8. Volcanic residue
9. Plate appearances
10. Reunion attendee
11. Alien's permission to work
12. Give permission to
13. 19th letter

Answers on page 169.

18. Forward sections of mezzanines
22. Nuisances
24. Garb for a girl
25. Lauds
26. Deodorant option
27. Transplant recipient
28. Use credit
30. Irritability
32. Hit the high points
33. Island in the Antilles
34. Ornament home?
36. Vacillates
38. Exposes
42. Veranda in Hawaii
44. Spirits
45. Cereal grass
47. Winter wool
49. Yippee!
50. Beyond requirements
51. VCR button
53. Golden calf, for one
55. Naval warfare branch: abbr.
56. President's nickname
57. Untrained
58. Yale grad
59. Exercise site

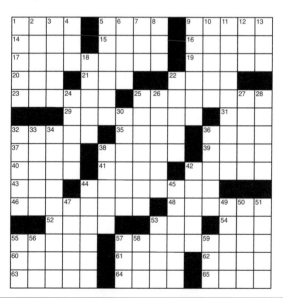

Founding Father Wisdom

Every word or phrase listed below is contained within the group of letters. Words can be found in a straight line horizontally, vertically, or diagonally. They may read either forward or backward. When complete, the leftover letters spell a seasonal quote from Benjamin Franklin.

CAROLERS

CHESTNUTS

CHRISTMAS

DANCER

DASHER

DECEMBER

EGGNOG

ELVES

EPIPHANY

FRANKINCENSE

FRUIT CAKE

JINGLE BELLS

JOLLY

JOY

LIGHTS

MISTLETOE

NATIVITY

NEW YEAR

PLUM PUDDING

PUMPKIN PIE

RUDOLPH

SANTA CLAUS

SHOPPING

SNOWMEN

STUFFING

WENCESLAS

WISE MEN

YULETIDE

Answers on page 169.

HIDDEN QUOTE:

_____

_____

```
A G O C H R I S T M A S O D G
E P I P H A N Y T I V I T A N
F S D C N E M W O N S E D N I
R T F O N Y U L E T I D E C F
U U S R O W C I H P E N C E F
I N D J A E C G N E E N E R U
T T I O S N I I O L G E M E T
C S S L L L K T A V O M B H S
A E H L C P E I O E N E E S R
K H O Y M L H N N S G S R A E
E C P U T T I N U C G I A D L
L C P S A L S E C N E W H R O
I S I S L L E B E L G N I J R
T M N S U A L C A T N A S M A
A S G N I D D U P M U L P E C
```

Code-doku

Solve this puzzle just as you would a sudoku. Use deductive logic to complete the grid so that each row, column, and 3 by 3 box contains each of the letters of the words JACK FROST.

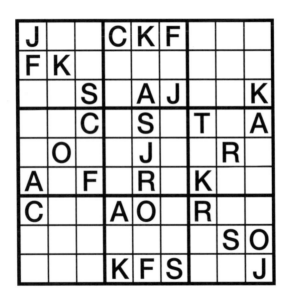

Ornamental

Find the one thing in common in each of the 8 rows of ornaments (vertically, horizontally, and diagonally).

Oh Christmas Tree!

Complete the word search to reveal a hidden message related to the puzzle's topic. Words can be found in a straight line horizontally, vertically, or diagonally. They may read either forward or backward. Once you find all the words, you can read the hidden message from the remaining letters, top to bottom, left to right.

ANGELS	HOLLY	REINDEER
BELLS	JOY	SANTA CLAUS
CANDLES	MAGI	SHEPHERDS
CHEER	MANGER	SINGING
CRECHE	MINCE PIE	SLEIGH
DECORATION	NATIVITY	SNOW
DINNER	NUTS	STAR
EGGNOG	PACKAGES	STOCKING
FEAST	PEACE	TINSEL
FROST	POINSETTIA	TRINKETS
GIFT	PRESENTS	TURKEY
GREETINGS	PUDDING	YULE

LEFTOVER LETTERS SPELL THE FIRST LINE OF A CHRISTMAS CAROL (5 WORDS).

```
                          G
                        J O Y
                  S E L D N A C
                      O G O
                L D K P H O L L Y
              E C A E P T R I N K E T S
                  I S L L E B G
              S I N G I N G A S N G M G
          Y T I V I T A N I I W E A E L U Y
                S E I M D T F N N
              S A N K A I C T G T U T E
            S S E T C L N N Y E K R U T S A S
      T S O R F G O A N G C R S N O W D S L E I G H
              T N E R E E D N I E R L O
            O S K R I E L P C I D E H C E R C
      G N I D D U P T S I H O H P A C K A G E S
  S A N T A C L A U S E E E E P O N O I T A R O C E D
                      E E U
                      H R T
                    S M A G I
```

Season's Greetings

Can you determine the missing letter in this logical progression?

D D P V C ___ D B

Holiday Anagram

What 2 words, formed by different arrangements of the same 6 letters, can be used to complete the sentence below?

At Christmas time in Bavaria, every _____ village displays a crèche scene with the baby Jesus lying in a _____.

Word Ladder

Change just one letter on each line to go from the top word to the bottom word. Do not change the order of the letters. You must have a common English word at each step.

GOLD

____

____

____

____

STAR

Christmas Tongue Twisters

Cryptograms are messages in substitution code. Break the code to read the message. For example, THE SMART CAT might become FVO QWGDF JGF if F is substituted for T, V for H, O for E, and so on.

1. GDPZ GDRRZ GEDRB GCK GTOO GEKK IDGC GDPBKO.
2. BTPGT'B OKDHC BODJKB UP BODLA BPUI.
3. AEDB AEDPHOK LOTFFKJ LEDBFOZ.

Answers on page 170.

Acrostic

Solve the clues below, and then place the letters in their corresponding spots in the grid to reveal a quote from Janice Maeditere. The letter in the upper-right corner of each grid square refers to the clue the letter comes from. A black square indicates the end of a word.

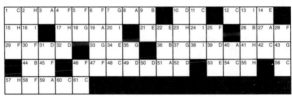

A. One of Santa's reindeer

___ ___ ___ ___ ___ ___ ___
27 3   8   51 19 40 59

B. Wash your mouth out with _____!

___ ___ ___ ___
9   26 44 36

C. Roasted snacks

___ ___ ___ ___ ___ ___ ___
1   56 48 11 42 12 54

___ ___
60 61

D. Yuletide pastime

___ ___ ___ ___ ___ ___ ___
39 50 31 52 10 49 32

E. Out and _____

___ ___ ___ ___ ___
21 22 53 34 14

F. Festive foliage

___ ___ ___ ___ ___ ___ ___
47 46 4   29 45 28 6

___ ___ ___ ___
25 30 58 5

G. Unverified bits of gossip

___ ___ ___ ___ ___ ___
37 18 7   33 35 43

H. Ceremonial candelabrum

___ ___ ___ ___ ___ ___ ___
17 57 41 23 55 15 2

I. "To grandmother's _____ we go."

___ ___ ___ ___ ___
20 13 24 16 38

Word Columns

Find the hidden quote from Andy Rooney by using the letters directly below each of the blank squares. Each letter is used once. A black square indicates the end of a word.

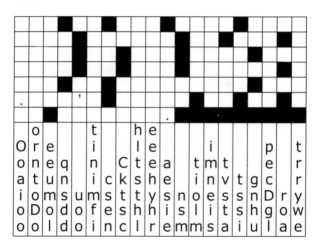

Spotlight on St. Nick

ACROSS

1. Garland and Blume
6. Umps' cohorts
10. This-and-that dish
14. A point ahead
15. Scat singer Fitzgerald
16. First-class
17. St. Nick's cargo
19. Cereal grasses
20. Govt. ecological watchdog group
21. Electric light
22. Stitched connection
24. Pigpen
25. _____ Paulo, Brazil
26. Formal headwear
29. St. Nick's place of business
31. New Zealand parrot
32. Contributors
35. Wordplay experts
37. Melville's "Typee" sequel
38. Carry with difficulty
39. Eye part
40. Landscaper
43. Formal, informally
45. A-Team member
46. St. Nick's team
48. Compounds of gurus
50. Tidal outflow
51. Multiply-curved wheel
54. Sit
55. With regard to
56. SHO rival
57. Winter white
59. A.k.a. St. Nick
62. Fireside yarn
63. Ancient Peruvian
64. Thicket of trees
65. Washstand pitcher
66. Satiric comic Mort
67. Blockheads

DOWN

1. Ferrer and Canseco
2. Inappropriate
3. Rot
4. Really big laugh
5. Promoter
6. Captured back
7. North Carolina university
8. Soar
9. Poet Siegfried
10. Songstress McLachlan
11. St. Nick's elves
12. Opposite of WSW
13. Unseld or Craven
18. Dreads
23. Omar of "House"

32   *Answers on page 171.*

26. Hired muscle
27. Hatcher and Garr
28. Smart-alecky
29. Potbelly fuel
30. Reject with distain
32. Religious tenet
33. Sharif and Bradley
34. St. Nick's whereabouts
36. Amphitheater level
38. Luau souvenirs
41. Notable periods
42. Goddess of vengeance
43. "Leap of Faith" star Winger

44. Daphne Du Maurier novel
47. Of the teeth
49. Oarsman
51. Cowboy leggings
52. Ill-treatment
53. Israelites' leader
55. ⅟₃₆ of a yard
57. Sault _____ Marie
58. Slangy turndown
60. Gasteyer of "Mean Girls"
61. _____ Angeles

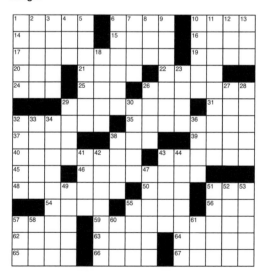

Here Comes Santa

The letters in TOYS can be found in boxes 7, 11, 15, and 20, but not necessarily in that order. Similarly, the letters in all the other words can be found in the boxes indicated. Your task is to insert all the letters of the alphabet into the boxes. If you do this correctly, the shaded cells will reveal another one of Santa's helpers.

Unused letters: J and Q

1	2	3	4	5	6	7	8	9	10	11	12	13

14	15	16	17	18	19	20	21	22	23	24	25	26
											Q	J

BLITZEN: 1, 8, 11, 12, 13, 22, 24

CHIMNEY: 3, 10, 12, 13, 15, 16, 22

ELVES: 8, 13, 18, 20

FAIRY LIGHTS: 4, 8, 10, 11, 12, 15, 19, 20, 21, 23

GROTTO: 4, 7, 11, 19

LAPLAND: 6, 8, 9, 22, 23

SANTA CLAUS: 5, 8, 11, 16, 20, 22, 23

SLEIGH: 8, 10, 12, 13, 19, 20

STOCKINGS: 7, 11, 12, 14, 16, 19, 20, 22

TOYS: 7, 11, 15, 20

VIXEN: 12, 13, 17, 18, 22

WHITE BEARD: 1, 2, 4, 6, 10, 11, 12, 13, 23

Code-doku

Solve this puzzle just as you would a sudoku. Use deductive logic to complete the grid so that each row, column, and 3 by 3 box contains each of the letters from the words JACK FROST.

					T			
	F			R				O
J	K		A					
O	R			C				J
		J		T		S		
C				S			O	A
					T		R	K
T				O			F	
		F						

Xmas Crossword

ACROSS

1. Lose color
5. Openhanded blow
9. Anglo-_____
10. Term of endearment
12. Scotch pine
15. Canned meats
16. Impolite
17. Unhappy
18. _____ Maria
19. In use
20. Bjorn _____
21. Continue despite opposition
23. Quick wash
24. Changed
26. To any extent
29. Let go
33. Tardy
34. Neat
35. Number of a Louis
36. Military mail-drop: abbr.
37. Waiter's handout
38. Do a clerk's job
39. Xmas custom
42. Vegas lights
43. School tests
44. Shower affection (on)
45. Matching pieces

DOWN

1. Food grower
2. Line of rotation
3. John _____ Passos
4. Give for safekeeping
5. Out of the sun
6. Misplace
7. Picnic pest
8. Individual
9. Use a razor
11. One's age
12. Fellow
13. Assembling, as troops
14. Border
19. Future law
20. Wait
22. Mall notice
23. Depend
25. Cuts back
26. _____ and alack
27. Make an easy putt
28. Expiated
30. Accepted truths
31. Door and window features
32. Preholiday times
34. Nervous

Answers on page 171.

37. Julep garnish
38. Campus group: abbr.
40. Muck
41. Woodsman's tool

Picture This

Place each of the 16 boxes in the 4 by 4 grid below so that they form a jingling holiday picture. Do this without cutting the page apart: Use only your eyes.

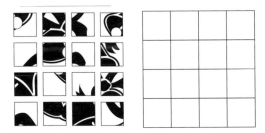

Ebenezer, in the Beginning

Cryptograms are messages in substitution code. Break the code to read the quote and attribution. For example, THE SMART CAT might become FVO QWGDF JGF if F is substituted for T, V for H, O for E, and so on.

AT! HDC TY EWB W CLPTC-KLBCYN TWIN WC
CTY PVLINBCAIY, BRVAAPY! W BZDYYULIP,
EVYIRTLIP, PVWBSLIP, BRVWSLIP, RXDCRTLIP,
RAFYCADB AXN BLIIYV!
—NLRQYIB, "W RTVLBCOWB RWVAX"

Acrostic

Solve the clues below, and then place the letters in their corresponding spots in the grid to reveal a quote from Erma Bombeck. The letter in the upper-right corner of each grid square refers to the clue the letter comes from. A black square indicates the end of a word.

A. Main character in "Miracle on 34th Street"

—— —— —— —— —— —— ——
41 54 12 22 14 71 3

B. Tree decorations

—— —— —— —— —— ——
63 20 55 40 49 42

—— —— ——
60 36 51

C. Wintertime construction

—— —— —— —— —— ——
47 57 9   39 52 50

——
35

D. Door adornment

—— —— —— —— —— ——
27 4   19 16 64 44

E. Time-honored practice

—— —— —— —— —— —— ——
32 45 67 61 70 1   25

—— ——
28 8

F. Youth

—— —— —— —— —— —— ——
43 24 6   30 17 11 53

—— ——
37 18

G. One who celebrates Christmas

—— —— —— —— —— ——
68 33 29 56 7   48

—— —— ——
21 34 13

H. "Silent _____"

—— —— —— —— ——
62 46 58 69 23

I. Recommendation for a juicy turkey

—— —— —— —— ——
65 38 15 10 66

J. Ran off quickly

—— —— —— —— —— ——
31 59 26 2   5   72

Answers on page 172.

Presents

ACROSS

1. Hydrant attachment
5. Get it wrong
8. Minor argument
12. Has a birthday
13. Floral neckwear
14. Unleavened bread
15. Christmas supply
18. Ethiopia's neighbor
19. Mare's morsel
20. Baseball stat
22. U.A.E. populace
27. More Christmas supplies
32. Part of HOMES
33. Fido's band
34. Concurrence
36. Nabisco treat
37. More Christmas supplies
39. Written passages
41. Hyson or pekoe
42. Cinder
44. Childhood taboos
49. Last of the Christmas supplies
54. Aroma
55. Half a natural 21
56. Fails to be
57. Tranquillity discipline
58. Butter portion
59. "_____ of the d'Urbervilles"

DOWN

1. Peddle by shouting
2. Fairy-tale monster
3. Oscar winner Penn
4. Catch a glimpse of
5. Whitney or Wallach
6. "Luncheon of the Boating Party" painter
7. Latvian capital
8. Health club
9. Die dot
10. Chowed down
11. Old sailor
16. Winter coat
17. Mom-and-pop grp.
21. Ice mass
23. Catnap
24. Surface size
25. Crooner Crosby
26. Matched collections
27. Glasgow gent
28. Ripped
29. Holm oak
30. Coagulate
31. Vault

Answers on page 172.

35. Position
38. Cornell's location
40. _____ Paulo, Brazil
43. Break suddenly
45. Final notice, briefly
46. Part of a muzzle
47. Has

48. Fast planes, for short
49. Siegfried's partner
50. Words at the altar
51. Peaty spot
52. Playtex product
53. Profit figure

Santa's Reindeer

Enter the names of Santa's reindeer into the grid, running
either across or down. Some letters are already placed,
and all words must interconnect.

O					C			S

BLITZEN	DONNER
COMET	PRANCER
CUPID	RUDOLPH
DANCER	VIXEN
DASHER	

Word Columns

Find the hidden quote from a silly holiday flyer by using the letters directly below each of the blank squares. Each letter is used once. A black square indicates the end of a word.

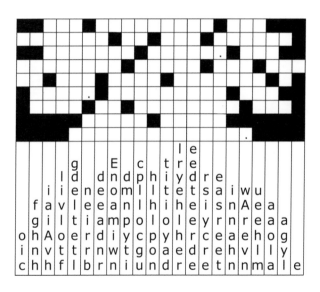

These Trees

Find the one thing in common in each of the 8 rows of ornaments (vertically, horizontally, and diagonally).

Say What?

Below is a group of words that, when properly arranged in the blanks, reveal a quote from Roy L. Smith.

under not heart who Christmas tree find

He _____ has _____ _____ in his _____ will
never _____ it _____ a _____.

Christmas Dinner Fit for a King

Cryptograms are messages in substitution code. Break the code to read the fun fact. For example, THE SMART CAT might become FVO QWGDF JGF if F is substituted for T, V for H, O for E, and so on.

ZW ISF PFHL 1213, MZWV UXSW XG FWVEHWY

XLYFLFY HQXKI ISLFF ISXKBHWY RHCXWB

(RSZRMFWB), H ISXKBHWY BHEIFY FFEB, GXKL

SKWYLFY SXVB, XWF SKWYLFY CXKWYB XG

HEDXWYB, HWY IOFWIP-GXKL RHBMB XG OZWF

GXL SZB SZB RSLZBIDHB GFHBI.

Picture This

Place each of the 20 boxes in the 7 by 4 grid below so that they form a picture of a holiday musician. Do this without cutting the page apart: Use only your eyes. Some boxes in the completed grid will be blank.

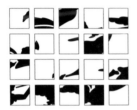

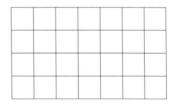

Christmas Cheer

Cryptograms are messages in substitution code. Break the code to read the message. For example, THE SMART CAT might become FVO QWGDF JGF if F is substituted for T, V for H, O for E, and so on.

"DIJMUQAVU BVPSU V AVYMD BVTG WPSJ
QIMU BWJCG, VTG HSIWCG, SPSJKQIMTY
MU UWRQSJ VTG AWJS HSVZQMRZC."
—TWJAVT PMTDSTQ XSVCS

Holiday Spell-doku!

This grid may look like a sudoku puzzle, but it uses letters instead of numbers. When the letters in each of the 9 mini-boxes are arranged in a certain way, they'll spell a holiday word or phrase.

H	U	B	A	K	N	T	E	H
U	M	G	T	I	C	L	B	E
A	B	H	S	N	I	E	H	M
E	S	C	E	O	R	O	S	E
T	A	E	O	N	P	I	M	L
R	D	O	L	H	T	T	E	T
I	T	S	H	A	C	R	M	O
K	G	O	T	I	S	A	N	T
N	C	S	M	S	R	S	E	N

Secret Santa

ACROSS

1. Feeble, as excuses go
5. Danger
10. Crimson Tide, briefly
14. Oil cartel
15. Swap
16. Steno's boss
17. Give it your all
19. Isn't wrong?
20. Kind of bath salts
21. Energizer
23. Green-lights
26. Spanish gold
27. Thomas the Tank Engine, e.g., to a tot
34. Stitch's friend
36. Cash's "A Boy Named ____"
37. Knitting tool
38. Prepare for battle, old-style
40. Rx writers
42. Punch dipper
43. Nike rival
45. Mil. men
47. Santa checks it twice
48. Said after a long trip
51. Feel poorly
52. Vital fluid
53. Great personal charm
58. Place to exchange rings
63. NBC's peacock, e.g.
64. Tot's riding toy
67. Melville captain
68. Goof
69. Horror-movie sounds
70. Extra
71. Campus bigwigs
72. Most excellent

DOWN

1. Balcony section
2. Each
3. Converted stables, in London
4. Canyon sound
5. ____ Club (onetime TV ministry)
6. Prior to
7. Cheerleaders' cries
8. "Same here!"
9. Manacle
10. Lady's man
11. Plant feature that sounds like a bar between wheels
12. It may drop down on your computer

Answers on page 173.

13. Isn't passive
18. Melville novel set in Tahiti
22. Roadside sleeper
24. Floors, briefly
25. Pond _____ (algae)
27. Allege
28. Mob or crowd
29. Row of bushes
30. Domain
31. "Paper Moon" girl _____ Loggins
32. Misfortunes
33. Nair rival
34. Remini of "The King of Queens"
35. _____-European (large language family)
39. Kenyan tribesman
41. Takes a load off
44. Rustled, as silk
46. _____ Na Na
49. "Freaky Deaky" author Leonard
50. Moonfish
53. Cherrystone, e.g.
54. Santa sounds hiding (separated) in this puzzle's long answers
55. Gelatin substitute
56. Judge's apparel
57. Magician's opener
59. Singer-songwriter Lisa
60. It has bark, but no bite
61. Makes inquiries
62. Take it easy
65. _____ mot
66. Mos. and mos.

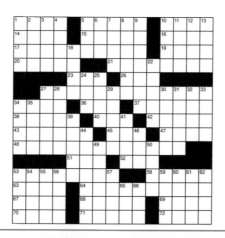

Where Is Christmas?

Christmas words have been removed from the words on the list. Write in the Christmas words to form the words that can then be found in the array of letters. Words can be found in a straight line horizontally, vertically, or diagonally. They may read either forward or backward.

_ _ _ _ _ _ UROUS

COW _ _ _ _ _

D _ _ _ _ _

DIS _ _ _ _ _

DOS _ _ _ EVSKY

EL _ _ _ N

EN _ _ _

EN _ _ _ _ _ _ E

ES _ _ _ _ _ E

F _ _ _ _ _ _

HABER _ _ _ _ _ _ Y

HOLE _ _ _ _ _ ER

_ _ _ _ CIAN

_ _ _ _ _ MAKER

MU _ _ _ _ D

RE _ _ _ _ _ _ ATIVE

_ _ _ _ _ _ T

S _ _ _ _ T

SU _ _ _ _

T _ _ _ _ _ O

_ _ _ _ _ ISH

W _ _ _ _ _

```
G H O L E P U N C H E R R P Y
Y E L O R A C S E D E P G O R
K S U O R U T N E V D A J N E
S I E H T A E R W N E N D M H
V Y D Q E E X L T D E L V E S
E V I T A T N E S E R P E R A
Y I S F T W T U M U S T A R D
O X C K L A P Y L L O H W Y R
T E A G C I N A I C I G A M E
S N R I N U G G S N P I G A B
O I D E Y V S H E U A E X K A
D S S S T R E E T L E L D E H
A H C O W B E L L S O S A R Q
```

Chilly Search

Every word listed is contained within the grid of letters. Words can be found in a straight line horizontally, vertically, or diagonally. They may read either forward or backward. Leftover letters spell a winter quote from Carl Reiner.

AVALANCHE

COLD SNAP

DRIFTS

FLAKES

FLURRIES

FREEZE

FROST

FROSTBITE

GALE

GLACIER

HOARFROST

ICE

ICICLE

NOR'EASTER

POWDER

RIME

SHIVERS

SLEET

SLUSH

SNOW

SNOWCAP

SNOWSTORM

SUBZERO

WHITEOUT

WINDCHILL

HIDDEN QUOTE:

_____

```
A L O S R E V I H S T O F P E
O P L W H I T E O U T E S R L
M S N O W C A P I K E F E S N
F R T N F R E E Z E O T I W R
R I O S L U S H F P S I R R E
O N D T O R E I C A L G R I D
S E T G S R T O E N B E U A W
T L N A U W F R N S A N L E O
C C E L E S O R S D A L F R P
Y I F E R N E N A L E Z A I N
G C M E T I B T S O R F O V F
W I N D C H I L L C H W A T A
R O R E Z B U S E K A L F E R
```

Picture This

Place each of the 16 boxes in the 5 by 5 grid below so that they form a picture of one of Santa's helpers. Do this without cutting the page apart: Use only your eyes. Some boxes in the completed grid will be blank.

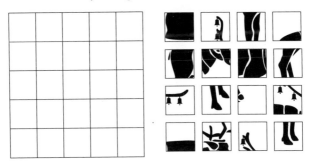

Holiday Gift

Cryptograms are messages in substitution code. Break the code to read the quote and its source. For example, THE SMART CAT might become FVO QWGDF JGF if F is substituted for T, V for H, O for E, and so on.

"POW IWCP JY XZZ TNYPC XEJSQG XQH
FOENCPRXC PEWW: POW AEWCWQFW JY X
OXAAH YXRNZH XZZ BEXAAWG SA NQ WXFO
JPOWE."
—ISEPJQ ONZZNC

Word Ladder

Change just one letter on each line to go from the top word to the bottom word. Do not change the order of the letters. You must have a common English word at each step.

COAL

_____

_____ water vessel

_____

_____

TOYS

Christmas Wordplay

There should be 5 words in the ladder below, but the third word is missing. The words are connected in some way. Which of these is the missing word? BANANA, CHOPPY, EATERY, FOLLOW, REPORT, OR ROOKIE?

MASCOT
CHALET

_____

NATURE
CLASSY

Webword

Using the letters found along the outside of the web, fill the empty spaces inside the web to create three 4-letter words running through the center of the web. One letter on the outside will go unused.

THEME: Winter

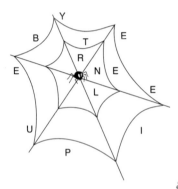

Toy Heaven

Can you assemble these letters in a way to spell a 2-word location from Christmas lore?

A H
K O T
O A S
S W P
R N S

Word Columns

Find the hidden quote from P. J. O'Rourke by using the letters directly below each of the blank squares. Each letter is used once. A black square indicates the end of a word.

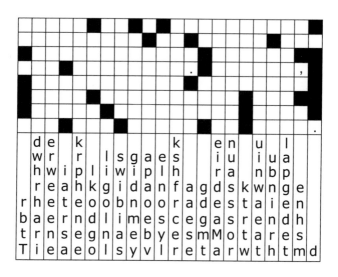

Word Jigsaw

Fit the pieces into the frame to form common words reading across and down. There's no need to rotate the pieces; they'll fit as shown, with each piece used once.

DR | CO / L | D / A / BIT | S / ITS | A / NEW | NY

IE / P | S / EAL | DU / DES | L / MAI | NG / G | U / IT

AR / R / NTR | OW | NT / E | IS | T / EFE | W / SPI

IE / T | R / END | H / UNT | N / E / TAP | HO / A | SO / W

A / WEB | E / REA | N / ING | SE / S | S / EE | P / BA

E / ND | T / IT | U / GI | LS | EC | SE / N

NI | ER

Christmas Acrostic

Solve the clues below, and then place the letters in their corresponding spots in the grid to reveal a quote from Agnes M. Pharo. The letter in the upper-right corner of each grid square refers to the clue the letter comes from. A black square indicates the end of a word.

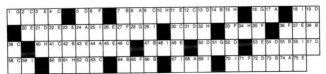

A. Fireplace

___ ___ ___ ___ ___ ___
8   24   44   74   17   68

B. Limo drivers

___ ___ ___ ___ ___ ___ ___
7   60   14   42   64   47   55

___ ___ ___
73   66   38

C. "All I want for Christmas is my two _____"

___ ___ ___ ___ ___ ___ ___ ___
30   9   41   58   12   39   63   46

___ ___
4   2

D. Space rocks, fallen to Earth

___ ___ ___ ___ ___ ___ ___
13   57   50   52   31   54   5

___ ___ ___
72   51   19

E. Granny and Poppa, to some

___ ___ ___ ___ ___ ___ ___
45   49   37   22   23   53   3

___ ___ ___ ___ ___
43   75   26   20   11

F. Baldness hiders

___ ___ ___ ___ ___ ___ ___
33   65   73   36   35   27   6

G. Prepares mashed potatoes, perhaps

___ ___ ___ ___ ___
1   51   16   62   28

H. Church singing groups

___ ___ ___ ___ ___ ___
40   34   61   10   32   15

I. Coldest

___ ___ ___ ___ ___ ___ ___
70   25   48   56   67   18   69

___ ___
29   59

Webword

Using the letters found along the outside of the web, fill the empty spaces inside the web to create three 4-letter words running through the center of the web. One letter on the outside will go unused.

THEME: Winter

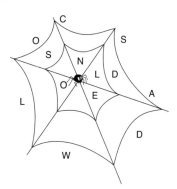

Say What?

Below is a group of words that, when properly arranged in the blanks, reveals a quote from Dale Evans.

time   action   Christmas   we   is   time

"Christmas _____ love in _____. Every _____ _____ love, every _____ we give, it's _____."

Gingerbread House

All the words listed below can be made from the letters in "gingerbread house." Words can be found in a straight line horizontally, vertically, or diagonally. They may be read either forward or backward. The leftover letters reveal a hidden message.

AIRBORNE

BEAR HUG

BEER GARDEN

BONEHEAD

BRAIN

BUDGERIGAR

BUGS

DEAR

DEBONAIR

DESIGNER

DIAGNOSE

DINOSAUR

DOGS

DRAB

EAGER

EERIE

GENEROUS

GREGARIOUS

HEROINE

HERRING

HUGE

NEIGHBOR

NERD

OGRE

RARE

RENEGADE

ROUGH

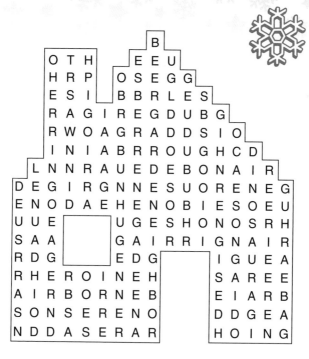

```
                  B
   O  T  H        E  E  U
   H  R  P     O  S  E  G  G
   E  S  I     B  B  R  L  E  S
   R  A  G  I  R  E  G  D  U  B  G
   R  W  O  A  G  R  A  D  D  S  I  O
   I  N  I  A  B  R  R  O  U  G  H  C  D
   L  N  N  R  A  U  E  D  E  B  O  N  A  I  R
D  E  G  I  R  G  N  N  E  S  U  O  R  E  N  E  G
E  N  O  D  A  E  H  E  N  O  B  I  E  S  O  E  U
U  U  E        U  G  E  S  H  O  N  O  S  R  H
S  A  A        G  A  I  R  R  I  G  N  A  I  R
R  D  G        E  D  G        I  G  U  E  A
R  H  E  R  O  I  N  E  H        S  A  R  E  E
A  I  R  B  O  R  N  E  B        E  I  A  R  B
S  O  N  S  E  R  E  N  O        D  D  G  E  A
N  D  D  A  S  E  R  A  R        H  O  I  N  G
```

Christmas Tunes

ACROSS

1. Chic and cool
5. Move like a cloud
9. Lion king
14. Punjabi princess
15. Slang for TV
16. Dotcom casualty of March 7, 2001
17. Ballpark figures: abbr.
18. Wields
19. "Buffalo Stance" singer Cherry
20. 1940 Irving Berlin song
23. Like a doily
24. Parts of a day: abbr.
25. "This way"
28. Met solo
30. 1989 play about Capote
33. Get together
34. Lyricist _____ Jay Lerner
35. Unfavorable picnic forecast
36. 1916 song by a Ukrainian composer
39. Hamburg's river
40. Colorado Indians
41. Draw forth
42. Canny
43. Ivan the Terrible, for one
44. Closer to 50-50
45. Sailor's yes
46. Fencers' match
47. Song first released by Bobby Helms in 1957
54. "The Thinker" sculptor
55. _____-Rooter
56. "The heat _____"
57. Former Attorney General Edwin
58. "Walkabout" director Nicolas
59. Big fashion magazine
60. Wet wintry mix
61. Nimble
62. A portion

DOWN

1. Got bigger
2. Whip
3. Naysayer
4. Kissing come-on
5. Wire-and-plaster wall covering
6. Like an easy job
7. Prefix with mensch
8. Lucy's partner
9. Nissan compact
10. Entries on a list

Answers on page 176.

11. Freeman of "Black Beauty"
12. Informal farewells
13. Blond shade
21. Painting support
22. Stand out
25. Henry R. and Clare Boothe
26. Counting everything
27. Baseball HOFer Puckett
28. Take in or let out
29. Cheerleaders' cries
30. Raptor's claw
31. Poet Rainer Maria ___
32. Al, Al Jr., or Bobby
34. Brut rival

35. Merrymaking activities
37. Small diving bird
38. Cut at an angle
43. Young swan
44. Funeral oration
45. Pernod flavoring
46. Discourage
47. "Piano Man" singer Billy
48. ___ fixe (obsessive thought)
49. Messes up
50. Cartoon Betty
51. Peace Prize city
52. Actor Meaney
53. Leg joint
54. Apt. units

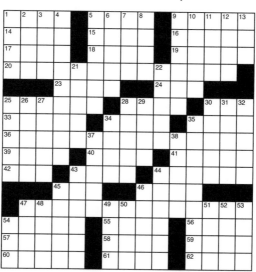

Christmas Message

Solve the clues below, and then place the letters in their corresponding spots in the grid to reveal a quote from Lorinda Ruth Lowen. The letter in the upper-right corner of each grid square refers to the clue the letter comes from. A black square indicates the end of a word.

A. Holiday sweets

___ ___ ___ ___ ___ ___ ___
27 7   60 26 21 70 55

___ ___ ___ ___ ___
66 41 72 36 12

B. Ark builder

___ ___ ___ ___
4   6   47 38

C. "The Little _____"

___ ___ ___ ___ ___ ___ ___
53 48 43 25 30 13 56

___ ___ ___
32 1   65

D. Difficult and dangerous feat

___ ___ ___ ___ ___
64 18 33 14 15

E. Yuletide wish

___ ___ ___ ___ ___ ___ ___ ___
9   11 39 19 31 50 40 71

___ ___ ___ ___
17 49 63 20

F. Partygoers

___ ___ ___ ___ ___ ___ ___ ___
10 74 73 69 44 46 8   16

G. Christmas dinner style, sometimes

___ ___ ___ ___ ___ ___
35 51 62 42 3   57

H. Like Ebenezer

___ ___ ___ ___ ___ ___ ___
34 58 68 22 54 37 5

I. Bring together

___ ___ ___ ___ ___
67 52 29 28 59

J. Like one who's had too much eggnog

___ ___ ___ ___ ___
24 61 2   23 45

Name Calling

Decipher the encoded words in the saying below using the numbers and letters on the phone pad. Remember that each number can stand for 3 or 4 possible letters.

Christmas isn't a 7-3-2-7-6-6, it's a 3-3-3-5-4-6-4.

1	2 ABC	3 DEF
4 GHI	5 JKL	6 MNO
7 PQRS	8 TUV	9 WXYZ
	0	

Answers on page 176.

Word Ladder

Change just one letter on each line to go from the top word to the bottom word. Do not change the order of the letters. You must have a common English word at each step.

SLED

_____

_____

_____ different colors

_____

_____ oversize

LUGE

How Big a Tree?

Cryptograms are messages in substitution code. Break the code to read the message. For example, THE SMART CAT might become FVO QWGDF JGF if F is substituted for T, V for H, O for E, and so on.

"WTRTS QNSSG MINLU UAT EZVT NC GNLS

XASZEUPME USTT. ZW UAT TGTE NC XAZDFSTW,

UATG MST MDD 30 CTTU UMDD."

—DMSSG QZDFT

Christmas Favorite

All the words in this puzzle are found in the famous Christmas poem, "'Twas the Night Before Christmas." Words can be found in a straight line horizontally, vertically, or diagonally. They may be read either forward or backward. The leftover letters reveal the name of the author.

ALL	HOUSE	SNUG
CHILDREN	JOLLY OLD	ST. NICK
CHIMNEY	ELF	THROUGH
CHRISTMAS	MERRY	TWINKLED
CREATURE	MOUSE	WHISTLE
DASH AWAY	ROOF	
DIMPLES	SLEIGH	

```
D F N E R D L I H C P
A L O T H R O U G H C
S E L P M I D E M R R
H D B S T N I C K I E
A L L Y W C C L H S A
W O E M I H H G U T T
A Y G U N S I O E M U
Y L R F K E M S N A R
T L O R L C N L T S E
H O U S E A E R K L E
R J M O D M Y O R E E
```

On the Tree

ACROSS

1. Online journals
6. Top gun
9. Show of deference
12. Yankee Yogi
13. Neighbor of Swed.
14. Segment of history
15. Talk-show host O'Brien
16. Sparklers for the tree
18. Lemon follower
19. Design with acid
20. Highland hats
22. Overhead RRs
23. Nile snakes
27. Hot temper
28. _____ Moines, IA
29. Bit of tomfoolery
30. Foil for the tree
32. Rival of the tree
33. River of Hades
34. Angora or Burmese
35. Lamb's father
36. "Lohengrin" lass
37. New Jersey cape
38. What's more
39. Tender cut
41. Wallach of "Lord Jim"
42. Loops for the tree
45. Snug
48. Lennon's widow

49. Part of AT&T
50. Sneeze sound
51. Coloring agent
52. Clod chopper
53. Stop gripping

DOWN

1. U.K. channel
2. Zodiac's only carnivore
3. Spheres for the tree
4. Alums
5. Compos mentis
6. Harpists for the tree
7. Young horses
8. _____ the Red
9. Wager
10. Lode load
11. Card game for two
17. Scottish feudal lord
20. Book ID
21. Disney mermaid
22. Lamprey
24. Topper for the tree
25. Gyro breads
26. Likable loser
28. Ruby of "A Raisin in the Sun"
29. Creative skill
31. "We _____ Overcome"
32. Manner
34. Light for the tree, once

37. Sal of "Rebel Without a Cause"
38. Wonderland visitor
40. Swear word
41. & others: Lat.

42. Zeus or Jupiter
43. Indefinite amount
44. Fish eggs
46. Glutton
47. Besides

1	2	3	4	5		6	7	8		9	10	11
12						13				14		
15						16			17			
		18				19						
20	21				22				23	24	25	26
27				28				29				
30			31				32					
33					34				35			
36				37				38				
			39	40				41				
42	43	44					45			46	47	
48				49			50					
51				52			53					

Word Jigsaw

Fit the pieces into the frame to form common words reading across and down. There's no need to rotate the pieces; they'll fit as shown, with each piece used once.

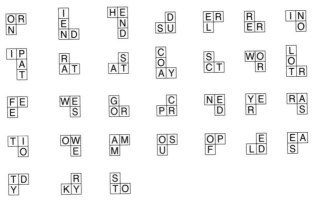

Christmas Acrostic

Solve the clues below, and then place the letters in their corresponding spots in the grid to reveal a quote from Grace Krilley. The letter in the upper-right corner of each grid square refers to the clue the letter comes from. A black square indicates the end of a word.

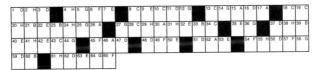

1 D	2 H	3 D	■	4 H	5 G	6 F	7 E	■	8 C	9 E	10 C	11 D	12 G	■	13 C	14 G	15 A	16 D	17 A	■	18 C	19 C
20 H	21 B	22 E	23 B	24 G	25 G	26 A	■	27 G	28 C	29 H	30 A	31 B	32 E	33 B	34 C	■	35 E	36 G	■	37 D	38 H	39 B
40 E	41 H	42 E	43 C	44 G	■	45 F	46 A	47 D	■	48 D	49 F	50 E	■	51 D	52 A	53 E	■	54 F	55 H	56 D	57 F	58 G
59 D	60 B	■	61 H	62 D	63 E	64 G	65 F															

A. Snapshots

___ ___ ___ ___ ___ ___
30   52   15   17   46   26

B. Togetherness

___ ___ ___ ___ ___
39   33   21   23   60

C. Incubator activity

___ ___ ___ ___ ___ ___ ___
28   13   8   18   19   10   43

___
34

D. Regrettable

___ ___ ___ ___ ___ ___ ___
16   11   48   1   59   51   47

___ ___ ___ ___
56   62   37   3

E. "It's lovely weather for a _____ together with you"

___ ___ ___ ___ ___ ___ ___
22   63   53   32   40   9   50

___ ___ ___
35   7   42

F. Festive

___ ___ ___ ___ ___ ___
54   49   45   6   57   65

G. Deliberately destroys

___ ___ ___ ___ ___ ___
27   25   14   5   36   58

___ ___ ___
12   64   44

H. Written studies on particular subjects

___ ___ ___ ___ ___ ___
24   49   2   38   4   20

___ ___ ___ ___
55   31   41   61

Word Columns

Find the hidden quote about Christmas by using the letters directly below each of the blank squares. Each letter is used once. A black square indicates the end of a word.

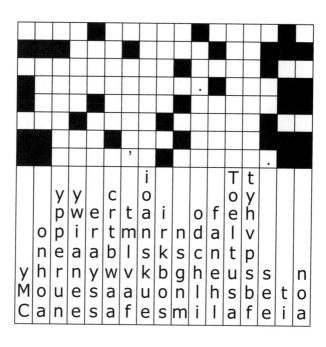

"The _____ before Christmas"

ACROSS

1. Fake tattoo, maybe
6. Start of an idea
10. Table of honor
14. Words before Paris or Lucy
15. Local yokel
16. Village People hit
17. "When what to _____ should appear..."
20. Cover with paint
21. Blood lines
22. Costa _____
25. Friday who said "Just the facts, ma'am"
28. Grammarian's concern
29. Get all histrionic
31. Matt of morning TV
33. Novelist Buntline
34. Folder material
36. Petting zoo favorite
38. "He was chubby and plump, a right _____"
41. Olympus competitor
42. Straight man
45. UCLA is one
48. They're bound to stay in place
50. Sleep sound
51. "You're _____!" ("You've had it!")
53. Positive votes
55. Secluded valley
56. Necessitate
58. Very small batteries
60. "Now, Dasher! Now, Dancer! Now, _____"
66. Split
67. Bath powder
68. Author Wharton
69. Falco of "Nurse Jackie"
70. Leer
71. Party hearty

DOWN

1. Not too brainy
2. Ron who played Tarzan
3. Moon jumper
4. Side interest
5. Jokester Jay
6. Fairy-tale girl
7. Continent north of Africa: abbr.
8. Slugger's stat: abbr.
9. Suvari of "American Beauty"
10. Some leather workers
11. "The Bonesetter's Daughter" author
12. When mammoths lived
13. Was impudent
18. Margery of nursery rhyme

19. Food lovers
22. "Shiny Happy People" band
23. "_____ little teapot..."
24. If, and, or but, briefly
26. "Hogwash!"
27. Bear alternative
30. Egg-shaped
32. George _____ of "CSI"
35. Seltzer starter
37. Next to
39. Lotus position discipline
40. Deceive
43. Test for college seniors: abbr.
44. Bard's nightfall

45. Vast grassland, especially of Russia
46. Hotelier Hilton
47. 1962 John Wayne film
49. Spirited session?
52. A votre _____!
54. In a funk
57. "My So-Called Life" actor Jared
59. Allege as a fact
61. Cloth scrap
62. Nothing but
63. 14, in old Rome
64. Vacation time for Henri
65. NY Rangers' org.

Christmas Morning

Unwrap the 12 differences between these 2 familial scenes.

Answers on page 178.

Acrostic

Solve the clues below, and then place the letters in their corresponding spots in the grid to reveal a quote from William Parks. The letter in the upper-right corner of each grid square refers to the clue the letter comes from. A black square indicates the end of a word.

1 C	2 G	3 G	4 G	5 H	6 B	7 A	8 C	9 B	■	10 J	11 E	■	12 B	13 J	14 C	15 D	16 H	17 I	18 D	■	19 J
20 E	21 B	22 D	■	23 F	24 H	25 D	26 A	■	27 F	28 C	29 F	30 C	31 G	32 C	33 E	■	34 H	35 A	36 B
37 I	38 H	■	39 A	40 C	41 H	42 E	43 F	44 J	■	45 A	46 E	47 I	48 G	49 H	50 I	51 H	52 C	■	53 D	54 E	55 I	56 C
57 G	■	58 B	59 A	60 E	61 D	■	62 B	63 F	■	64 E	65 J	66 D	■	67 E	68 A	69 I	70 E	71 I

A. Accidents

__ __ __ __ __ __ __
7 68 39 35 59 45 26

B. _____ of the Christ
(Mel Gibson film)

__ __ __ __ __ __ __
58 21 5 9 36 62 12

C. Organizations remembered
during the holiday season

__ __ __ __ __ __ __
1 40 8 56 32 14 30

__ __
52 28

D. Nervous

__ __ __ __ __ __ __
15 25 18 61 53 66 22

E. Second-day-of-Christmas gifts

__ __ __ __ __ __ __
6 42 60 33 67 46 20

__ __ __ __
64 54 70 11

F. Rice _____

__ __ __ __ __
29 23 43 27 63

G. Gift from the Magi

__ __ __ __ __
48 57 3 31 2

H. Snowstorm condition

__ __ __ __ __ __
34 38 4 24 49 41

__ __
16 51

I. Cold-weather wraparounds

__ __ __ __ __ __
17 37 50 47 69 55

__
71

J. Sound signal

__ __ __ __ __
19 65 44 10 13

Answers on page 178.

The First Christmas

The letters in GOLD can be found in boxes 10, 14, 15, and 18, but not necessarily in that order. Similarly, the letters in all the other words can be found in the boxes indicated. Your task is to insert all the letters of the alphabet into the boxes. If you do this correctly, the shaded cells will reveal the names of 2 very important people.

1	2	3	4	5	6	7	8	9	10	11	12	13
												Q
14	15	16	17	18	19	20	21	22	23	24	25	26

BETHLEHEM: 4, 5, 15, 20, 22, 26

CENSUS: 1, 9, 19, 20, 23

DONKEY: 8, 9, 10, 18, 20, 24

FRANKINCENSE: 1, 3, 6, 7, 9, 12, 19, 20, 24

GOLD: 10, 14, 15, 18

JESUS: 17, 19, 20, 23

MYRRH: 5, 7, 8, 22

NAZARETH: 4, 6, 7, 9, 20, 22, 25

OX: 2, 18

SAVIOR: 3, 6, 7, 11, 18, 19

SHEPHERDS: 7, 10, 19, 20, 21, 22

WISE MEN: 3, 5, 9, 16, 19, 20

Word Columns

Find the hidden quote from Robert Louis Stevenson using the letters directly below each of the blank squares. Each letter is used only once. A black square indicates the end of a word.

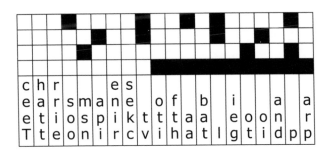

Word Ladder

Change just one letter on each line to go from the top word to the bottom word. Do not change the order of the letters. You must have a common English word at each step.

GIFT

_____

_____ underground growth

_____

_____

_____ talk donkey talk

_____

_____

WRAP

Word Jigsaw

Fit the pieces into the frame to form common words reading across and down. There's no need to rotate the pieces; they'll fit as shown, with each piece used once.

Santa's Grotto

There are 17 things wrong with this scene. See if you can
be Santa's helper and find them all!

Tasty Scramblegram

Four 6-letter words, all of which revolve around the same theme, have been jumbled. Unscramble the 4 words and write the answers in the space next to each one. Next, transfer the letters that are in the shaded boxes into the empty spaces below and unscramble the 8-letter word that goes with the theme.

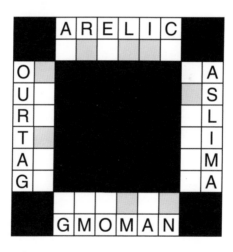

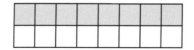

Well-Loved Carols

ACROSS

1. Kudzu, e.g.
5. "Could you repeat that?"
9. Save opposite
14. Soviet sub class
15. Tip-top
16. Like zoo animals
17. Certain mystical Muslim
18. Carry
19. Writer Horatio
20. Christmas carol: Latin
23. Put money on
24. _____ gratia artis
25. "Mercy!"
28. Angry
30. Brief life story
32. Shoe box letters
33. Arctic outerwear
35. Legal drama that featured the Venus Butterfly
37. Christmas carol
40. Yokels
41. Relax
42. Program interrupters
43. Do-say link
44. Lend an ear
48. It has a thumb but no fingers
51. Gore and Jolson
52. Hubbub

53. Christmas carol
57. Parade sponsor since 1924
59. Great N.Y. gallery
60. Bud of "Harold and Maude"
61. De Gaulle's birthplace
62. Like good steaks
63. Plinth
64. Paragon
65. It smells great
66. Spotted

DOWN

1. Sushi condiment
2. Escape artist
3. Sissified
4. Speaker's platform
5. ABBA's first hit
6. _____ it (goes by foot)
7. Voting no
8. Prepared for a drive
9. Reptilian, in a way
10. "Ancient" prefix
11. Omelet maker's discard
12. Born, in French
13. Old initials for East Germany
21. Rides
22. Punk rock offshoot
26. Hearty drink made with honey

27. Archery wood
29. Actress Emerson
30. "One planet" religion
31. Alibi _____ (excuse makers)
34. Numbered rds.
35. _____ May Alcott
36. Some Dada works
37. Oscar-winner Dench
38. Roadblock
39. Not shoddy
40. Shofar source
43. A few or a lot
45. Nobel-winning Bengali poet Rabindranath

46. Channel swimmer Gertrude
47. Sitcom sewer worker
49. Dancer-choreographer Tharp
50. Canvas stand
51. Willie of "Paradise"
54. Somalian-born model who wed David Bowie
55. NASA nix
56. Sergeants, for instance: abbr.
57. 1051, in old Rome
58. Helping hand

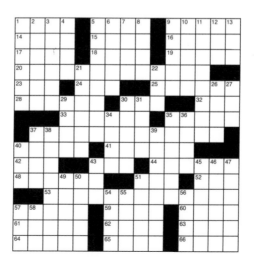

Word Ladder

Change just one letter on each line to go from the top word to the bottom word. Do not change the order of the letters. You must have a common English word at each step.

SING

_____

_____

_____

_____ many denials

NOEL

Sound of Silence?

Cryptograms are messages in substitution code. Break the code to read the message. For example, THE SMART CAT might become FVO QWGDF JGF if F is substituted for T, V for H, O for E, and so on.

ZERP XN QGCB'N XT BGP MEEO QXBG
JED CB FGMXNBOCN XW JED NBEA
EAPTXTK AMPNPTBN CTY ZXNBPT.
—CDBGEM DTVTEQT

Let It Shine

Move each of the letters below into the grid to form common words. You will use each letter once. The letters in the numbered cells of the grid correspond to the letters in the phrase at the bottom. Completing the grid will help you complete the phrase and vice versa. When finished, the grid and phrase should be filled with valid words, and you will have used all the letters in the letter set.

Hint: The numbered cells in the grid are arranged alphabetically, so the letter in the cell marked 1 will appear in the alphabet before the letter in the cell marked 2, and so on.

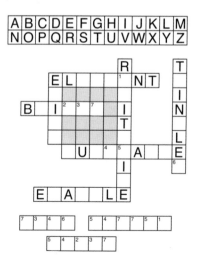

Presents for Kids

Every word listed is contained within the group of letters. Words can be found in a straight line horizontally, vertically, or diagonally. They may be read either forward or backward. Leftover letters spell out a hidden phrase.

AIR RIFLE

BALL

BICYCLE

BLOCKS

CANDY CANE

CHECKERS

CHEMISTRY SET

DOLLS

ERECTOR SET

FRISBEE

HOBBYHORSE

JACK-IN-THE-BOX

JACKS

JUMP ROPE

KITE

MARBLES

MODEL AIRPLANE

MODEL TRAIN

SCRABBLE

SLINGSHOT

SLOT CAR

TOY TRUCK

YO-YO

```
T O H S G N I L S N B N R O T
H X O B E H T N I K C A J I N
E N A C Y D N A C G C A L E I
E R E C T O R S E T C O S L A
E S M S E T A N O K A S L B G
P I V R L I N L S L L O D B G
O C H E M I S T R Y S E T A A
R C D K F M H I L D S O M R E
P O T C H R A T O Y T R U C K
M O D E L A I R P L A N E S I
U N T H G U S S B I C Y C L E
J I E C F U L F B L O R O C H
K R A I R R I F L E E I S Y T
M H O B B Y H O R S E S A S O
```

93

Christmas Songs

Every word listed below is contained within the group of letters. Words can be found in a straight line horizontally, vertically, or diagonally. They may read either forward or backward.

AWAY IN A MANGER

DECK THE HALLS

THE FIRST NOËL

JINGLE BELLS

JOY TO THE WORLD

THE LITTLE DRUMMER BOY

O CHRISTMAS TREE

O COME, ALL YE FAITHFUL

O HOLY NIGHT

SILENT NIGHT

SILVER BELLS

WE THREE KINGS

WHAT CHILD IS THIS?

WHITE CHRISTMAS

WINTER WONDERLAND

S G N I K E E R H T E W S F W X I S D T
T W F N G M E L L G U I D H P Z L T E S
G H E R X L N U X P L I A X Z B C R M A
H B E X D L R O W E H T O T Y O J P B M
Q K G L B L M W N T C M L X K T L W D T
Y E G N I C J T I H Z X E N E Z K N R S
L E D S P T N I I J K X S S O J A Q E I
Z L E O L I T L N U U U D R X L N L G R
K I R R G L D L D G N U S S R Z E U N H
L U F H T I A F E Y L L A E M O C O A C
Z C T F S S Z H U D L E D R N V O G M E
E G B T D I A E E E R N B T N H L F A T
N V H M Z V X M B H O U S E O J Z K N I
C I P V B J M R T W T R M L L Y G Y I H
S S J D T Z E G R S I K Y M J L E A Y W
L D W D G V X E A F I N C U E X S D A C
P Q A R L G T I E Z I R P E X R H Y W Y
A B W I L N Y H Y G J I H M D O B D A O
L A S H I F T U H I B J V C Q W R O P R
T K O W C L D T H E V R E P O D B U Y I

Word Jigsaw

Fit the pieces into the frame to form common words reading across and down. There's no need to rotate the pieces; they'll fit as shown, with each piece used once.

```
O        S        R I P      E        P O D      D S
N S      A C E             O D        L
         R                            T

A T      C O      W        S        L A      S
  E             S E      C U T       L A      I T
                         G          T

  V      A T        N      B A      A        S A
M I      R        M E N             R N        A N
                    G

U E        I      M        B E      P        R O
R        A L      E A               S I         T

L        T        A R E    O N T
L O T    S T        E
```

Christmas Tree

Every word listed is contained within the group of letters. Words can be found in a straight line horizontally, vertically, or diagonally. They may read either forward or backward. The leftover letters reveal a holiday sentiment.

BLITZEN	NOËL
CARDS	PRANCER
CAROLS	PRESENTS
COMET	SCROOGE
CUPID	STOCKINGS
DANCER	TINSEL
DECK THE HALLS	TINY TIM
DONDER	TREE
EGGNOG	VIXEN
ELVES	XMAS
HOLLY	YULE LOG

```
              T
            D S H
            I   L E
          B P L E E
          P U A G C
        E R C H G O S
        B E A E N M T
      T L S R H O E S Y
      U I E O T G T L P
    N E T N L K O T I R M
    E D Z T S C L R H A I
    X E E S K E E O E N T
  D I L N I O D L E C C Y X
  O V R N N N L U A T E N M
  E I G O O Y S Y N I R I A
  S S S S D R A C T O B E T S D
              R
            W R O E A
            T H O E D
            I N G A S
            M I E L E
```

Food for Thought

Every word listed is contained within the group of letters. Words can be found in a straight line horizontally, vertically, or diagonally. They may read either forward or backward.

APPETIZER

BLEND

BOUILLON

CASSEROLE

CHEESE

COCKTAIL

DRIED BEEF

FRENCH ONION

FRUIT

GARNISH

GOURMET

GRAPEFRUIT

GUACAMOLE

HERB

JUICE

PASTA

RELISH

SALAD

SAUCE

SPICE

TOMATO

```
L M K F J R F E E B D E I R D
T B Z G O U R M E T P B D T G
G L K K B O U I L L O N R C U
C R S A U C E E C I U J H R A
N N A L T L Q O Y H N S F E C
L O Y P K C C K E A I X N Z A
J L I G E K A R S N T L P I M
L H F N T F B S R P K S D T O
C Z M A O C R A S R I A A E L
H B I H T H G U J E L C D P E
E L C S I T C Q I A R N E P C
E X W I U F R N S T E O R A M
S B V L R W N V E L T T L M Z
E G G E F C H J B R R N B E M
Q F N R O T A M O T F Z X Q W
```

Say What?

Below is a group of words that, when properly arranged in the blanks, reveal a quote from Bob Hope.

> find glow great simplest Christmas we recall things happiness

When we _____ _____ past, _____ usually _____ that
the _____ _____—not the _____ occasions—give off
the greatest _____ of _____.

Noel

Find the word "noel" once—and only once—in the word grid below.

```
L O E N N O L O
O O N O L O L N
E N O N O N E E
L E N O E E O N
N O L O N O O L
O L N O E N N L
L E O L E L E O
E N E L O L E N
```

Stargazer

Look closely at these 15 stars. While they all may appear identical at first, you'll find they're really not. Divide the stars into six groups of identical stars: Group I will contain four stars; Groups II and III will each contain three stars; Groups IV and V will each contain two stars; and Group VI will contain the only unique star.

Christmas at the Movies

ACROSS

1. Peck, for one
5. Humpback herds
9. Gives off coherent light
14. Dutch treat
15. Others, to Octavian
16. Taper off
17. Philosopher Descartes
18. Skip a turn
19. "_____ out!"
20. 1970 film based on a Nesbit novel, with "The"
23. Thee and _____
24. Generic John
25. Ring surface
28. Have a fowl diet?
32. Grave letters
35. Bring a smile to
37. Drops from the sky
38. Zola heroine
39. 1996 movie with Arnold Schwarzenegger
42. "I'll get right _____."
43. Not taped
44. What's happening
45. "Arabian Nights" menace
46. Actress Hudgens of "High School Musical 2"
48. Prepare to drag
49. Used a stool
50. Had a little lamb
52. 1987 Yuletide classic starring Keshia Knight Pulliam, with "The"
61. Battlezone maker
62. Michelle of "Crouching Tiger, Hidden Dragon"
63. Track event
64. Wee bits
65. Branch headquarters?
66. The real Popeye Doyle
67. Hang around
68. Emcee
69. Deep-six

DOWN

1. "Galloping Gourmet" Graham
2. Sneaking suspicion
3. _____-Flush
4. Silvery food fish
5. Fruit with a musky tang
6. Oil of _____
7. Music buy
8. Robe closer
9. Hide
10. Dwelling
11. Dino's tail?
12. French 101 verb

Answers on page 182.

13. No longer hidden
21. Potter's need
22. "_____ know" ("Beats me")
25. Big-time
26. Essential acid
27. Costume for "I, Claudius"
29. Get into condition
30. Have a little cow
31. Annoys
32. Less cooked
33. Like some chatter
34. Premium channel
36. Bilko, e.g.
38. Ariz. neighbor
40. Gladden
41. Ledger of "A Knight's Tale"
46. Overnight bag
47. Fragrant packet
49. Watchband
51. Everglades wader
52. _____-back (relaxed)
53. "Believe _____ not"
54. Breezy sendoff
55. Old story
56. Sleek, in car lingo
57. Low digits
58. Othello's treacherous ensign
59. Some VCRs
60. Camera part

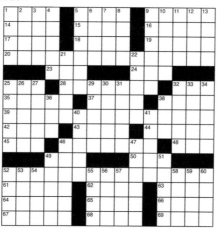

Picture This

Place each of the 18 boxes in the 6 by 4 grid below so they form a picture of a gracious gifter. Do this without cutting the page apart. Six boxes will remain blank.

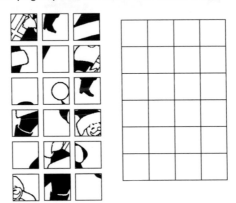

Singer's Dream

Cryptograms are messages in substitution code. Break the code to read the quote and its source. For example, THE SMART CAT might become FVO QWGDF JGF if F is substituted for T, V for H, O for E, and so on.

"EJALCC SL TZXL YRMUCITZC ZJ KYYZCUKJ

IK CRZML KEM PALCCUJFC, ZAA IRL CJKS UJ

ZAZCXZ SKJ'I TZXL UI 'SRUIL.'"

— PUJF YMKCPG

Ornaments (Part I)

Study these illustrations for one minute then turn the page for a memory challenge.

Nutcracker

Santa

Reindeer

Elf

Candy cane

Sled

Snowman

Sleigh bell

Santa's sleigh

Ornaments (Part II)

Do not read this until you have read the previous page!

Circle the words you saw illustrated on the previous page.

Santa

Stocking

Angel

Elf

Snowman

Globe

Toboggan

Picture frame

Reindeer

Sleigh bell

Word-a-Maze: Iced Orbs

Travel in sequence through the puzzle from the left side to the right, using each numbered clue to determine the correct word. Connect adjacent words together with a common letter to proceed through the maze. Some letters are already given. The first and last words tie into the title.

1. Winter storm

2. Famous bread

3. Ran fast

4. State of limited function

5. Famous Mark

6. Bird home

7. Waist treatment

8. Small suitcase

9. Grills

10. Supplies

11. Done alone

12. Peace birds

13. Dog command

14. Kernel support

15. Fancy dances

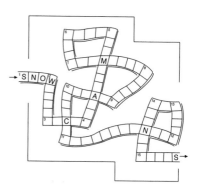

Answers on page 183.

Ornament

Fit the pieces into the frame to form common words reading across and down. There's no need to rotate the pieces; they'll fit as shown, with each piece used once.

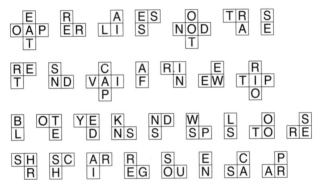

What's in a Name? Ask Santa

ACROSS

1. A Simpson
5. Docile
9. Miserly
14. Blessing
15. _____ Mountains (Eurasia divider)
16. Basket twig
17. Fair and square
18. Phone opener
19. Type of violet
20. Santa to some in the Netherlands
23. Brood
24. It's west of Africa: abbr.
25. White collar crime
27. Pal of Francois: Fr.
29. Swelled head
32. Labor leader's cry
33. Let it stand, in proofreading
34. Delhi dress
35. Santa in England
38. San Diego's _____ Mesa
39. Native Oklahoman
40. Pizza slice
41. Puncture sound
42. ER hookups: abbr.
43. Wash lightly
44. Night school subject: abbr.
46. "Titanic" sinker
47. Santa to some in Russia
53. Gas meter, for one
54. Fashion reporter Klensch
55. Mil. addresses
57. Landed
58. Horse halter
59. Everybody, down South
60. Rock with crystals inside
61. House title
62. Open carriage

DOWN

1. JFK's VP
2. Markers
3. Slugger Sammy
4. Aversion
5. "Now, now!"
6. Nicer than "ain't"
7. Timbuktu's land
8. Major utility: abbr.
9. Go _____ (deteriorate)
10. Tony Bennett's "This _____ I Ask"
11. "Dennis the Menace" girl
12. Dame Myra
13. Give it a go
21. Checking account type

Answers on page 183.

22. Half of Hispaniola
25. Tiny bugs
26. Wilson and Moreno
27. Pal of Aramis
28. No more than
29. Chair designer Charles
30. Say it before dinner
31. River near Paris
32. Area 51 vehicles, in lore
33. "SNL"-like Canadian comedy
34. Some Corvettes
36. Stirs up
37. He served between Hubert and Gerald
43. Send back to a lower court
44. Trimmed landscape
45. Like Elvis's shoes
46. Count of music
47. Small fish
48. Two-tone coin
49. Do a sheepdog's job
50. Bauhaus artist Paul
51. Brightly colored food fish
52. "Nana" author
53. Joke
56. Foxy

Word Columns

Find the hidden quote from Shirley Temple by using the letters directly below each of the blank squares. Each letter is used once. A black square indicates the end of a word.

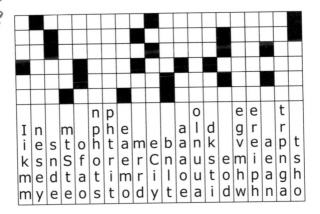

Santa

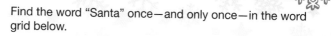

Find the word "Santa" once—and only once—in the word grid below.

```
A N S A T N A N T S
T A A S A N N T T A
N S N A A A N T A S
A A N A S T S A N T
N N A N S A T S T N
S A T T A N T A N T
S T S A A S N N T A
A A N S A T S N S T
T N T A T A A T N A
A S A N A S N A A S
```

Riddle

The past Christmas Day was on a Friday. The past New Year's Day was also on a Friday, exactly 7 days later.

In the year 2022, Christmas Day and New Year's Day will fall on different days of the week. What is the reason for this?

Answers on page 184. **115**

Deck the Halls

ACROSS

1. Wild swine
5. Starbucks order
10. Rice-A-_____
14. Crucifix letters
15. Guardian spirit
16. "Think nothing _____!"
17. The first L in L.L. Bean
18. Small branch
19. "There was an old lady who swallowed _____"
20. "Deck the halls with . . ."
23. Suffix with humor
24. Ages and ages
25. "Tell me something _____ know"
28. Rathskeller glass
30. Bearing
33. Old Mideast political union: abbr.
34. Samuel Pepys, for one
37. Government bureau
38. "Troll the ancient . . ."
41. Smidgen
42. Fruit rich in vitamin C
43. Coll. entrant's stat
44. Schooner support
45. Expressed disapproval
49. Conductor Zubin
51. MC's need, for short

53. Dutch piano center
54. "Strike the harp and . . ."
59. Poet Khayyam
61. In the know
62. Machu Picchu builder
63. Häagen-_____
64. Singer Frankie
65. Tournament ranking
66. Pasta used in soups
67. Site of the Krupp steelworks
68. Word in a threat

DOWN

1. A hobbit and his namesakes
2. "Two to go" situation
3. Stir to action
4. Anchor part
5. Cow catcher
6. Playwright Chekhov
7. Happy weekend acronym
8. Word in many college names
9. City of northeast Nevada
10. Author Dahl
11. "Time to leave"
12. Zilch
13. Theatrical suffix
21. Figure skater Sonja
22. Architect Maya
26. Scientist's sprinkle
27. Attempt
29. Between jobs

Answers on page 184.

30. In the _____ of (surrounded by)
31. Shrink's remark
32. Leave one's mark?
35. Procter & Gamble razor brand
36. Jamaica's Ocho _____
37. Jean's sculptures
38. Cry of pain
39. Musical NBA team
40. Eighth letter, spelled out
41. Leo is its logo
44. Spring time in Paris
46. Bit of corn
47. Draws out
48. Noted libertine
50. Tailor's dummy, e.g.
51. Singer Haggard
52. Freeze closed, as some harbors
55. Cathedral area
56. "_____ brillig. . ."
57. Dutch painter Franz _____
58. River from Ardennes to the Seine
59. Constable _____ ("Star Trek: Deep Space Nine")
60. Spoil

Picture This

Place each of the 24 boxes in the 5 by 6 grid below so they form a picture of a beloved gift. Do this without cutting the page apart: Use only your eyes.

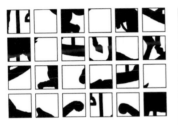

Decorations

Plug in the appropriate 7 consonants to find the word.

O A E A I O

Word Columns

Find the hidden book excerpt and its author by using the letters directly below each of the blank squares. Each letter is used only once. A black square indicates the end of a word.

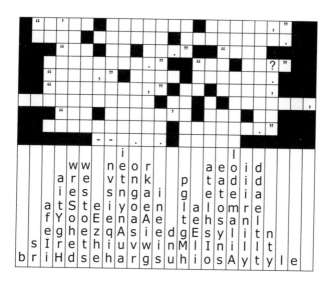

Snowflake

Fit the pieces into the frame to form common words reading across and down. There's no need to rotate the pieces; they'll fit as shown, with each piece used once.

Picture This

Place each of the 12 boxes in the 3 by 4 grid below so they form a picture of a winter treat. Do this without cutting the page apart.

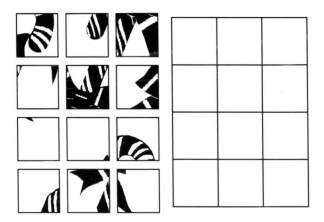

Word Ladder

Change just one letter on each line to go from the top word to the bottom word. Do not change the order of the letters. You must have a common English word at each step.

STAR

_____

_____

_____

_____

_____

TREE

Christmas Mix-Up

Can you rearrange the letters in these words to form 4 Christmas titles?

1. TRUANT CHECKER

2. LIGHTEST INN

3. HE GOT FIFTIETH MAG

4. FUND OF WATER LILIES

Answers on page 185.

Colorful Scramblegram

Four 6-letter words, all of which revolve around the same theme, have been jumbled. Unscramble the 4 words and write the answers in the space next to each one. Next, transfer the letters that are in the shaded boxes into the empty spaces below and unscramble the 8-letter word that goes with the theme. The theme for this puzzle is color shades.

| R | E | I | C | E | S |
| | | | | | |

L					M
I					A
V					D
E					K
R					A
S					S

| | | | | | |
| | I | N | S | A | N | E |

Word Ladder

Change just one letter on each line to go from the top word to the bottom word. Do not change the order of the letters. You must have a common English word at each step.

SNOW

_____

_____

_____ Cut of pork

_____

_____

CAPS

The Three Kings

The 3 kings are on their way to Bethlehem. Guide them through the maze to their destination.

Answers on page 185 and 186.

Christmas Crossword

ACROSS

1. Furthermore
4. Go bad
7. Gives a hoot
12. Halloween scare word
13. "_____ we there yet?"
14. Grown-up
15. "Frosty the _____"
17. "I Saw _____ Kissing Santa Claus"
18. Make a boo-boo
19. Copier filler
21. La Scala production
23. Sunrise direction
27. Granny
29. Healthful retreat
31. Dove's call
32. "_____ Bells"
34. "_____ Night"
36. Industrious bug
37. Took a seat
39. Many Little League coaches
40. Red veggie
42. Religious ceremonies
44. Name on a deed
46. Baltic or Mediterranean
49. "_____ Christmas"
52. "_____ the Red-Nosed Reindeer"
55. Ran on TV
56. "Green" prefix
57. Loser to Grant
58. Wine glass parts
59. Comfy room
60. Marketing pieces, briefly

DOWN

1. Tummy muscles, for short
2. "_____ of your beeswax!"
3. Way in or out
4. Ewe's mate
5. Give a speech
6. Some saxes
7. Showed up
8. Be crazy about
9. Molasses-based liquor
10. Shade tree
11. Porker's home
16. Incorrect
20. Quick snoozes
22. Chums
24. Got a perfect score on
25. Cain and Abel, to Adam
26. Little tyke
27. Golf course half
28. Start the poker pot
30. Assistant

Answers on page 187.

32. Sharp punch
33. Make, as a salary
35. Rodeo rope
38. In layers, like a wedding cake
41. _____ pole (tribal carving)
43. Break in hostilities
45. Ties the knot

47. Fitzgerald of jazz
48. Did an impression of
49. "Now . . . where _____ I?"
50. Broadway success
51. Ill temper
53. Mob head
54. "For _____ a jolly good . . ."

Christmas Tree

Fit the pieces into the frame to form common words reading across and down. There's no need to rotate the pieces; they'll fit as shown, with each piece used once.

OOM	T	S	OP	L	E	L
R	OR	TE	A	KI	DDL	I

N	B	RIF	DR	E	EL	S
PT	REA	F	O	DR	Y	SE
						E

L	P	RI	OUD	LO	U	
DIP	CO	IL	T	T	PU	

SE	V	C	AM	R	L	DE
R	ET	CA	Y	UN	FA	E

E	WO	UI	SA	LL	E	DS
SA	A	S	LT	S	S	

Silent Night

Looks like old St. Nick slipped some differences into this scene. Can you find all 16?

Trees & Stars

Find the hidden ornamental star for each Christmas tree in the grid. There is one star connected to each tree either horizontally or vertically. Stars don't touch each other, not even diagonally. Numbers outside the grid reveal the total number of stars in the corresponding row or column. We've placed one to get you started.

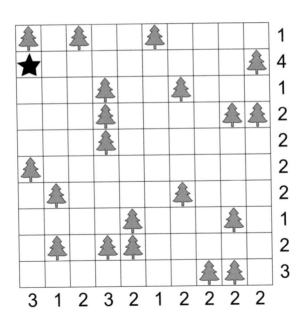

Acrostic

Solve the clues below, and then place the letters in their corresponding spots in the grid to reveal a quote from Helen Keller. The letter in the upper-right corner of each grid square refers to the clue the letter comes from. A black square indicates the end of a word.

1 F	2 H	3 D		4 A	5 D	6 E	7 H		8 C	9 H	10 B	11 C	12 H		13 B	14 D	15 I	16 F	17 H	18 A		19 F
20 C		21 E	22 I	23 B	24 C	25 F	26 D	27 B	28 D	29 G	30 D	31 C	32 D	33 B		34 D	35 B		36 C	37 E		38 D
39 I	40 F		41 E	42 G	43 A		44 E	45 B	46 I		47 E	48 G	49 A	50 D	51 F	52 F	53 A	54 I	55 G		56 H	57 B
	58 G	59 C	60 I		61 B	62 A	63 B	64 D	65 B											

A. Church address

___ ___ ___ ___ ___ ___
43 62 49 53 4   18

B. Scrooge, for one

___ ___ ___ ___ ___ ___ ___
27 10 35 63 57 65 61

___ ___ ___ ___
23 45 13 33

C. Restrain

___ ___ ___ ___ ___ ___ ___
31 11 36 59 8   24 20

D. Christmas season

___ ___ ___ ___ ___ ___ ___
38 34 5   26 14 64 30

___ ___ ___
50 32 3

E. Grip tightly

___ ___ ___ ___ ___ ___
47 6   37 44 21 41

F. Glass-clinking moments

___ ___ ___ ___ ___ ___
1   40 19 16 52 25

G. Persian potentates

___ ___ ___ ___ ___
55 58 42 48 29

H. "Happy _____!"

___ ___ ___ ___ ___ ___
2   17 9   56 12 28

___ ___
7   51

I. Move about wildly

___ ___ ___ ___ ___ ___
46 22 15 54 60 39

Answers on page 187.

Star of David

Fit the pieces into the frame to form common words reading across and down. There's no need to rotate the pieces; they'll fit as shown, with each piece used once.

```
GOA    T      T      W      ITY    EE
 P     IV    OA     TED      E      D

H      N      L      EE     C      BAR
IN    ATA    LO      A      ET      S

ER    ERS    H      RE     ES      M
 N     E    MOL      V      D      RE

 C     S     PA     IX      B
SHO    ID     T      L      RE

DO    ITE     N     SI      T
 D     O     DER     B     MA
```

Winter Wonders and Woes

Every word listed is contained within the grid of letters. Words can be found in a straight line horizontally, vertically, or diagonally. They may be read either forward or backward.

BLACK ICE

ICICLE

MELTING

PLOW

POTHOLES

SALT

SHOVELING

SKATING

SLEET

SLUSH

SNOW ANGELS

SNOWBALL

SNOWMAN

SUBZERO

WINDCHILL

```
S  K  N  G  J  H  J  B  S  S  R  E  F  T  G
E  R  V  V  S  P  L  W  N  S  M  R  S  Y  G
C  B  S  Y  P  A  G  O  L  I  R  Z  Y  K  N
I  V  R  I  C  K  W  U  P  M  M  W  M  F  I
B  N  S  K  W  A  S  W  S  A  D  F  I  M  T
Z  U  I  N  N  H  Q  S  A  X  R  G  L  E  A
T  C  V  G  O  R  E  Z  B  U  S  Q  L  L  K
E  E  E  A  G  W  R  P  T  B  P  I  I  T  S
C  L  E  M  Z  J  M  D  K  S  O  C  H  I  S
S  E  P  L  L  X  P  A  A  G  T  I  C  N  A
G  D  Y  I  S  A  H  L  N  A  H  C  D  G  M
C  S  E  Y  E  A  T  N  K  S  O  L  N  D  K
S  H  O  V  E  L  I  N  G  B  L  E  I  D  Z
B  A  Q  H  X  Q  V  N  T  K  E  X  W  W  Q
Z  L  L  A  B  W  O  N  S  N  S  P  L  O  W
```

Words Found in "Christmas"

Every word listed is contained within the grid of letters.
Words can be found in a straight line horizontally,
vertically, or diagonally. They may be read either forward
or backward.

AITCH	CRAMS	SCHIST
AMISH	CRASH	SCRAM
AMISS	CRASS	SCRIM
ASTIR	HAIRS	SHIRT
CARTS	HARMS	SITAR
CASTS	MARCH	SMART
CHAIR	MARSH	STAIRS
CHARM	MASTIC	STARCH
CHARS	MATCH	TRASH
CHART	MIRTH	TRIMS
CHASM	MISCAST	TSARISM
CHATS	SCHISM	

```
G Z P M S W A K T S I H C S I
I S K M D M M E I K M R P R T
A T A N S V I I N W A R I R R
V R D I S F S C R S F T A V Y
C A H K M Z H L H T S S C H A
A C H A I R B S Y A H Z S B E
S T S A R I S M S C R S W T M
T M S M T L D H R A I S P A S
S F A A R W I A S M R F R C A
A U B R C R T R A I T C H H H
S S N S T S I T A R S A N A C
M R A H C A I T H C T A M R J
M A R C H T S M A S T I C T I
```

Say What?

Below is a group of words that, when properly arranged in the blanks, reveal a quote from Robert Kirby.

you they lights matter snarled stored

No _____ how carefully _____ _____ the _____ last year, _____ will be _____ again this Christmas."

Addagram

This puzzle functions exactly like an anagram with an added step: In addition to being scrambled, each word or phrase below is missing the same letter. Discover the missing letter, then unscramble the words. When you do, you'll reveal 4 traditional wedding anniversary gifts (of various levels).

LEAP

VEILS

LEAD ME

SLY CAT

What's the Missing Word?

The missing words in the holiday song titles can be found in the grid. They may be in a straight line horizontally, vertically, or diagonally, and either forward or backward.

1. "ALL I WANT FOR CHRISTMAS IS MY TWO FRONT _____"
2. "_____ THE HALLS"
3. "_____ THE SNOWMAN"
4. "_____ GOT RUN OVER BY A REINDEER"
5. "HAVE YOURSELF A _____ LITTLE CHRISTMAS"
6. "I SAW _____ KISSING SANTA CLAUS"
7. "I'LL BE _____ FOR CHRISTMAS"
8. "JINGLE _____"
9. "JINGLE BELL _____"
10. "LET IT _____!"
11. "RUDOLPH THE _____ REINDEER"
12. "THE LITTLE _____ BOY"
13. "WINTER _____"
14. "THE _____ DAYS OF CHRISTMAS"
15. "_____ CHRISTMAS"

```
R E V L E W T R U M Q
T E E T H O X R U M P
U M M I S N O W P U D
M O T O C D C U R F E
T E W E H E F N L Y S
A M D N A R G O N L O
R O C K O L D M L E N
T M I S M A E E S B D
N M T T H N B R C E E
L Y I P T D L R E K R
D R U M M E R Y F T Y
```

Food

ACROSS

1. Klutzes
5. Stag, doe, and fawn
9. Lady of the house
12. Movie
13. _____ of Wight
14. Lupino or Tarbell
15. Heavy holiday dessert
17. Negative link
18. Future fish
19. Condemn openly
21. Carrier bags
24. "...parsley, sage, rosemary, and _____"
26. Ultimate degree
27. Jack or Joker
29. Hot tubs
32. Pitchblende or galena
33. Aids a criminal
35. Cold cubes
36. Laundry
38. Jeans-maker Strauss
39. Opposite of WSW
40. Subdues
42. Modern surgical tool
44. Stocking stuffer
46. Martino and Pacino
47. Gehrig or Costello
48. Red-and-white delight
54. Aesop's industrious insect
55. Natural soother
56. Outback gem
57. Nod of the head
58. Hoses down
59. Hanoi holidays

DOWN

1. Slightly askew
2. Melodic tune
3. Grippe
4. Affected smile
5. Gambling cubes
6. NASA's ISS partner
7. Antlered creature
8. Thin-voiced
9. Spicy holiday desserts
10. Olfactory stimulus
11. Nativity figure
16. Puccini opera
20. Ambulance initials
21. Christmas forecast
22. Gillette shaver
23. Open-fire roasters
24. Christmas decorations
25. New tube letters
28. Up to the task
30. Complexion woe
31. Soothsayer

34. Half-baked
37. Ten-gallon item
41. Raucous parrot
43. Wide necktie
44. Rub out
45. Top-rated
46. Citrus coolers

49. Flagon filler
50. _____ on your life!
51. Orangutan or gibbon
52. _____ "King" Cole
53. Golfer Ernie

1	2	3	4		5	6	7	8		9	10	11
12					13					14		
15				16						17		
			18					19	20			
21	22	23				24	25					
26				27	28				29		30	31
32				33			34		35			
36			37		38					39		
	40		41				42	43				
44	45					46						
47				48	49	50				51	52	53
54				55				56				
57				58				59				

Christmas Time

Every word listed is contained within the grid of letters. Words can be found in a straight line horizontally, vertically, or diagonally. They may be read either forward or backward.

BETHLEHEM

CANDLES

CAROLERS

CHESTNUTS

CHIMNEY

DASHER

DECEMBER

DECORATIONS

EPIPHANY

FRANKINCENSE

GREETINGS

HOLIDAY

MANGER

MISTLETOE

POINSETTIA

REINDEER

SLEIGH

SNOWMAN

STABLE

STOCKING

TINSEL

WASSAILING

WREATH

YULETIDE

```
C W N L W M E H E L H T E B P
H Z I G R E E T I N G S O V O
E Y G N I K C O T S N U T Z I
S N O I T A R O C E D S E M N
T A S L E C C X C A N D L E S
N H R I N D H N E L B A T S E
U P K A A T I N S E L X S L T
T I G S W K M T H U H R I Z T
S P H S N R N Z E G E S M B I
M E J A N U E H O L I D A Y A
R A R W I O Y A O T U E B H Y
U F N U A Q W R T F U Y L Z L
Z Q H G B S A M S H H K N S X
R E B M E C E D A W D Y K V F
Z B R B Q R R E I N D E E R C
```

Word Columns

Find the hidden quote from Hamilton Wright Mabie by using the letters directly below each of the blank squares. Each letter is used once. A black square indicates the end of a word.

```
n     w h a     w       r s       i v
w l e r e e h d     i n     l o e             h o
s h o s s c d y o     o l g a g e s s e c e o
B p i l i c y o e f d t h n e a t a s n
```

NORTH POLE

Christmas Presents

The letters in RAZOR can be found in boxes 11, 14, 23, and 25, but not necessarily in that order. Similarly, the letters in all the other words can be found in the boxes indicated. Your task is to insert all the letters of the alphabet into the boxes. If you do this correctly, the shaded cells will reveal a place where you could buy some of your Christmas presents.

1	2	3	4	5	6	7	8	9	10	11	12	13
14	15	16	17	18	19	20	21	22	23	24	25	26
		Q										

AFTERSHAVE: 1, 7, 8, 9, 10, 18, 23, 25

BOOK: 11, 17, 24

CUFF LINKS: 2, 3, 6, 7, 9, 13, 15, 17

DIARY: 6, 20, 23, 25, 26

FOUNTAIN PEN: 1, 2, 6, 7, 8, 11, 12, 13, 23

GIN: 5, 6, 13

JEWELRY: 1, 4, 15, 19, 20, 25

PERFUME: 1, 2, 7, 12, 21, 25

RAZOR: 11, 14, 23, 25

SHIRT: 6, 8, 9, 10, 25

VODKA: 11, 17, 18, 23, 26

WHISKEY: 1, 4, 6, 9, 10, 17, 20

XBOX: 11, 22, 24

Answers on page 189.

Decorating the Tree

All the words listed below can be made from the phrase "decorating the tree." Words can be found in a straight line horizontally, vertically, or diagonally. They may be read either forward or backward. The leftover letters reveal a hidden message.

ADHERENT

ADORE

ANGER

ANTIC

CARTRIDGE

CHEERING

COHERENT

CREATOR

DICTATOR

DRAGON

EIGHTEEN

ENERGETIC

GARDENER

GRACE

HERITAGE

HEROINE

INTERROGATE

NECTAR

NEGOTIATE

ORNATE

REACTION

RETICENT

TEENAGER

TOGETHER

C
C H O
S I E R A
I N T E N T B
E R A
O G I T R
N C R N E T E
E I R E G E N G F
A C T E N E N E A I S
N A E E C C T
R E T G E D I I H
I T C O D O E T R D G
W I T T R I G R E E H T I
H E I I A E R N V R H N T E E
A G R A T N O T E O I
T O T C C R D I N G T R O
E N O E N T A D H E R E N T R
O F T A N T I C H T R N E C I H E
R D I C T A T O R H T E E N A G E R H
N E I D H
R S R T O
M A A S C
G T R E E

Say What?

Below is a group of words that, when properly arranged in the blanks, reveal a quote from Bernard Manning.

kids once included toys with batteries bought

I _____ _____ my _____ a set of _____ for Christmas _____ a note on it saying, '_____ not _____.'

Age-Old Question

Next year I will be 21 but just 2 days ago I was 18. Hard to believe? There is only one day of the year—my birthday—that could make my opening statement true. What day is my birthday, and on what day did I make this statement?

Window Shopping

Find the 16 things wrong with this Christmas shopping scene!

Answers on page 190.

Word Columns

Find the hidden quote from Tom Sims by using the letters directly below each of the blank squares. Each letter is used once. A black square indicates the end of a word.

Decorations (Part I)

Study these illustrations for one minute, then turn the page for a memory challenge.

Plastic Santa

Lights

Holly

Garland

Ornaments

Angel

Snow globe

Stocking

Tree

Decorations (Part II)

Do not read this until you have read the previous page!

Circle the words you saw illustrated on the previous page.

Stocking

Mistletoe

Santa

Garland

Ribbon

Ornaments

Angel

Popcorn strands

Lights

Presents

Tree

Webword

Using the letters found along the outside of the web, fill the empty spaces inside the web to create three 4-letter words running through the center of the web. One letter on the outside will go unused.

THEME: Jesus' birth

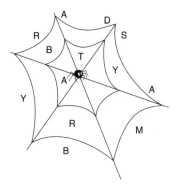

Say What?

Below is a group of words that, when properly arranged in the blanks, reveal a quote from Charles Schulz.

something someone doing little

"Christmas is _____ a _____ _____
    extra for _____."

Name Calling

Decipher the encoded word in the quote from Dale Evans below using the numbers and letters on the phone pad. Remember that each number can stand for 3 or 4 possible letters.

"Christmas is 5-6-8-3 in action."

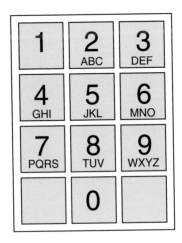

Magic Tree

Start at the top of the Christmas tree and find your way down to the bottom, moving between neighboring ornaments. Each letter from A to R must be used exactly once on the way.

A B C D E F G H I
J K L M N O P Q R

What Can You Fit in a Christmas Stocking?

What words, that is. How many words can you make from the letters in STOCKING? Here are some clues:

1. Royal ruler _____

2. Liquid in a pen _____

3. Change in your pocket _____

4. What a skunk may do _____

5. You might tie one _____

6. Purchase from the market _____

7. Enter your John Hancock _____

8. Perform at a karaoke bar _____

9. Skeleton's covering _____

10. Clock sound _____

Holiday Wordplay

There are 14 letters in "Merry Christmas." But if you count each different letter just once, there are only 10 unique letters. Can you rearrange those 10 letters to form a high school subject and the top grade a good student would get in it?

Word Columns

Find the hidden quote from Dave Barry by using the letters directly below each of the blank squares. Each letter is used once. A black square indicates the end of a word.

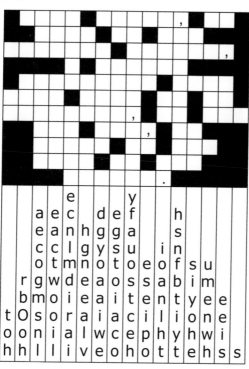

Santa's Helpers

ACROSS
1. Half a Disney duo
6. Drops at dawn
9. Splatter protector
12. O'Connor's successor
13. Y sporter
14. Beehive State native
15. Tim who played Santa Claus in "The Santa Clause"
16. Leslie who played Santa Claus in "Santa Who?"
18. Uses the touch system
20. Convenience store convenience: abbr.
21. "Breaking Bad" network
24. Can't take
26. Deceive
29. Sprite in "The Tempest"
32. Edward, who played Santa Claus in "Elf"
33. Sebastian, who played Santa Claus in "Miracle on 34th Street"
35. Veronica of "Hill Street Blues"
37. Saudi's neighbor
38. Remark to the house
40. "No dice!"
41. Buffet table server
43. "Myra Breckinridge" novelist
46. Lloyd, who played Santa Claus in "In the Nick of Time"
48. Tom, who played Santa Claus in "The Polar Express"
52. Was on a slate
53. Welder type
54. "Silas Marner" novelist
55. Long in the tooth
56. Party invitation initials
57. 1975 Barry Manilow hit

DOWN
1. Sound from the lea
2. Pipe fitting
3. Be off one's feet
4. Margin marking
5. Upscale
6. Star in Cygnus
7. Otis, the elevator man
8. Links prodigy Michelle
9. Big contract failure
10. Tidbit of gossip
11. Bernanke of the Fed
17. Will Rogers prop
19. Pipes-playing god

21. Patterned after
22. Jersey material
23. Water-to-wine site
25. Black and white predator
27. Part of an economics pair
28. Vein extractions
30. Israel's Abba
31. Petty or Loughlin
34. Scalpers' items, slangily
36. Car-for-hire company
37. Logician's abbr.

39. Studio 54, for one
41. Range that extends to the Arctic Ocean
42. Stilton cheese feature
44. Attention getter
45. In _____ land (spacey)
46. "Don't tase me, _____!"
47. Salesman's "gift"
49. "Delta of Venus" author
50. Pounded senseless
51. Place for a trough

Holiday Puzzler

The five two-word phrases below all relate to Christmas, but we've made a few changes. First, we removed the same letter from each word. Then, we jumbled the remaining letters. Your job is to figure out what letter's missing from each side and put it on the center line. For example, if you saw EYU ___ GO, you might realize that an L is missing from both sides. When you add the L to both words, they can unscramble to spell YULE LOG. When read from top to bottom, the missing letters in the center will spell out another Christmas-related word.

LERHAC _____ ENCKDI

STMSHRCI _____ ROLSC

TAIS _____ KIC

NIY _____ MI

NIOPETTSI _____ NTLP

Merry Scrambled Christmas!

Can you rearrange the letters in these terms to make Christmas-related terms?

1. MISS CHATTERER

2. NEWS ITEM HERE

3. VENETIAN'S CITY

Festive Fare

The letters in CAKE can be found in boxes 11, 14, 20, and 21, but not necessarily in that order. Similarly, the letters in all the other words can be found in the boxes indicated. Your task is to insert all the letters of the alphabet into the boxes. If you do this correctly, the shaded cells will reveal another Christmas food item.

1	2	3	4	5	6	7	8	9	10	11	12	13
14	15	16	17	18	19	20	21	22	23	24	25	26

CAKE: 11, 14, 20, 21

CHORIZO: 1, 3, 6, 12, 14, 19

CRANBERRY SAUCE: 8, 9, 11, 14, 18, 19, 21, 22, 26

CUSTARD: 2, 8, 11, 14, 17, 18, 19

GATEAUX: 11, 16, 17, 18, 21, 24

HAM: 1, 11, 25

JELLY: 5, 21, 22, 23

MINCE PIES: 8, 9, 12, 14, 15, 21, 25

PLUM PUDDING: 2, 5, 9, 12, 15, 18, 24, 25

SQUASH: 1, 8, 11, 13, 18

STRAWBERRIES: 8, 10, 11, 12, 17, 19, 21, 26

STUFFING: 7, 8, 9, 12, 17, 18, 24

VEGETABLES: 4, 5, 8, 11, 17, 21, 24, 26

ZUCCHINI: 1, 6, 9, 12, 14, 18

Answers on page 192.

Oh Christmas Tree

Every word listed is contained within the grid of letters. Words can be found in a straight line horizontally, vertically, or diagonally. They may read either forward or backward.

ANGELS

BELLS

BOWS

BULBS

CANDLES

CANDY CANES

CRECHE

GARLAND

GIFTS

GINGERBREAD

ICICLES

LIGHTS

MISTLETOE

NATIVITY

NUTCRACKER

ORNAMENTS

PINE

POPCORN

PRESENTS

RIBBONS

SANTA

SNOW

STAND

STAR

TINSEL

TOYS

TREE

WREATH

```
L U Z S S T S Q L I G H T S S
Q E R U E O W Y T I V I T A N
C O S Q L G O X P F G N P R N
B T N N C G B R I I E E O E E
R E O R I B B O N S G H P K F
S L W F C T I G E A T T C C X
U T T X I X E R R N M A O A B
S S A J R R P L B G D E R R U
T I N N B V A P V E D R N C L
O M D R D N M P T L L W J T B
Y S E L D N A C L S I L R U S
S A N T A U C R E C H E S N R
D P C A N D Y C A N E S Y D M
```

White Christmas (page 4)

The leftover letters spell: "To perceive Christmas through its wrapping becomes more difficult with every year."

Picture This (page 7)

Twisted Path (page 6)

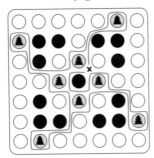

Word Ladder (page 8)

YULE, mule, mute, lute, luge, lugs, LOGS

Anagram (page 8)

1. Santa Claus; 2. North Pole; 3. ornaments; 4. wise men

Wacky Wordy (page 7)

Noel (No L)

Holiday Cheer (page 9)

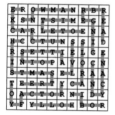

Christmas Tamagram (page 10)

Blameless (same bells)

Too Many Santas (page 10)

There are 158 "Santas" in the grid.

Happy Christmas (page 11)

1	2	3	4	5	6	7	8	9	10	11	12	13
G	H	Y	T	I	N	S	E	L	P	B	O	D
14	15	16	17	18	19	20	21	22	23	24	25	26
V	X	W	Z	U	M	A	J	K	Q	C	F	R

The Heart of Christmas (page 12)

The leftover letters spell: "He who has not Christmas in his heart will never find it under a tree."

Word Columns (page 14)

Oh look, yet another holiday TV special! How touching to have the meaning of Christmas brought to us by cola, fast food, and football.

Say What? (page 15)

"Santa Claus has the right idea. Visit people once a year."

One Time (page 15)

```
F E L L F F E
E L E F E F L
L E F L L F E
L F L F E F E
F L F E F E L
E F (E L F) L L
L E F E L E F
```

Word Ladder (page 16)

Answers may vary. REIN, vein, veil, veal, deal, dear, DEER

St. Nick's Sidekicks (page 16)

Santa Claus has some colorful companions in European countries. They include the limping, soot-covered Knecht Ruprecht; the French Père Fouettard, a sinister character who carries whips; the scary-looking Krampus of Austria and nearby countries; and the fur-wearing Belsnickel of Germany and Pennsylvania Dutch country, who may leave a lump of coal in the stockings of naughty children!

Snowed-Men (page 17)

1. scarf; 2. buttons; 3. 3 coal buttons; 4. arms up; 5. only 2 pieces, body and head; 6. button nose; 7. hats; 8. carrot nose

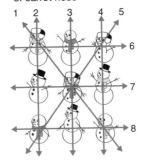

Hiding Some Christmas Things (page 18)

Red and Green (page 20)

Code-doku (page 24)

Founding Father Wisdom (page 22)

The leftover letters spell: "A good conscience is a continual Christmas."

Ornamental (page 25)

1. rows of dots; 2. two pairs of thick and thin lines; 3. wave pattern; 4. hearts; 5. snowflakes; 6. paisley; 7. all upside down; 8. stars

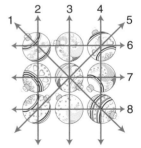

Oh Christmas Tree! (page 26)

The leftover letters spell: "Good King Wenceslas looked out."

Season's Greetings (page 28)

The missing letter is C, as in "Cupid." The sequence: Dasher, Dancer, Prancer, Vixen, Comet, Cupid, Donner, Blitzen

Holiday Anagram (page 28)

German/manger

Word Ladder (page 29)

Answers may vary. GOLD, goad, road, roar, soar, STAR

Christmas Tongue Twisters (page 29)

1. Tiny Timmy trims the tall tree with tinsel.

2. Santa's sleigh slides on slick snow.

3. Kris Kringle clapped crisply.

Acrostic (page 30)

"Christmas is not as much about opening our presents as opening our hearts."

A. Prancer; B. soap; C. chestnuts; D. singing; E. about; F. poinsettias; G. rumors; H. menorah; I. house

Word Columns (page 31)

"One of the most glorious messes in the world is the mess created in the living room on Christmas day. Don't clean it up too quickly."

Spotlight on St. Nick (page 32)

Xmas Crossword (page 36)

Here Comes Santa (page 34)

1	2	3	4	5	6	7	8	9	10	11	12	13
B	W	M	R	U	D	O	L	P	H	T	I	E

14	15	16	17	18	19	20	21	22	23	24	25	26
K	Y	C	X	V	G	S	F	N	A	Z	Q	J

Code-doku (page 35)

Picture This (page 38)

Ebenezer, in the Beginning (page 38)

Oh! But he was a tight-fisted hand at the grindstone, Scrooge! a squeezing, wrenching, grasping, scraping, clutching, covetous old sinner!
—Dickens, "A Christmas Carol"

Acrostic (page 39)

A. Kringle; B. ornaments; C. snowman; D. wreath; E. tradition; F. childhood; G. Christian; H. night; I. baste; J. dashed

"There is nothing sadder in this world than to awake Christmas morning and not be a child."

Presents (page 40)

Santa's Reindeer (page 42)

R		C	U	P	I	D			B			
U					A				L		D	
D		V	I	X	E	N			I		A	
O						C	O	M	E	T	S	
L					E				Z		H	
P	R	A	N	C	E	R			E		E	
H							D	O	N	N	E	R

Word Columns (page 43)

All employees are invited to the annual holiday party. All children under the age of ten will receive a gift. Employees who have no children may bring their grandchildren.

These Trees (page 44)

1. stand; 2. garland; 3. lights; 4. ornaments; 5. candles; 6. angel topper; 7. star topper; 8. presents

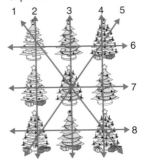

Say What? (page 45)

"He who has not Christmas in his heart will never find it under a tree."

Christmas Dinner Fit for a King (page 45)

In the year 1213, King John of England ordered about three thousand capons (chickens), a thousand salted eels, four hundred hogs, one hundred pounds of almonds, and twenty-four casks of wine for his Christmas feast.

Picture This (page 46)

Christmas Cheer (page 46)

"Christmas waves a magic wand over this world, and behold, everything is softer and more beautiful."
—Norman Vincent Peale

Holiday Spell-doku! (page 47)

From left to right in each row: Bah, humbug; Saint Nick; Bethlehem; decorates; North Pole; mistletoe; stockings; Christmas; ornaments

Secret Santa (page 48)

Where Is Christmas? (page 50)

advent; bells; elves; cards; toy; eve; joy; wreath; carol; lights; dasher; punch; magi; merry; star; present; sleigh; tree; pine; angel; vixen; holly

```
G H O L E P U N C H E R R P Y
Y E L O R A C S E D E P G O R
K S U O R U T N E V D A J N E
S I E H T A E R W N E N D M H
E V I T A T N E S E R P E R A
Y I S F T W T U M U S T A R D
O X C K L A P Y L L O H W Y R
T E A G C I N A I C I G A M E
S N R I N U G G S N P I G A B
O I D E Y V S H E U A E X K A
D S S S T R E E T L E L D E H
A H C O W B E L L S O S A R Q
```

Chilly Search (page 52)

Leftover letters spell: "A lot of people like snow. I find it to be an unnecessary freezing of water."

```
A L O S R E V I H S T O F P E
O P L W H I T E O U T E S R L
M S N O W C A P I K E F E S N
F R T N F R E E Z E O T W R
R I O S L U S H F P S R R E
O N D T O R E I C A L G R I D
S E T G S R T O E N B E U A W
T L N A U W F R N S A N L E O
C C E L E S O R S D A F R P
Y I F E R N E N A L E Z A I N
G C M E T I B T S O R F O V F
W I N D C H I L L C H W A T A
R O R E Z B U S E K A L F E R
```

Picture This (page 54)

Holiday Gift (page 54)

"The best of all gifts around any Christmas tree: the presence of a happy family all wrapped up in each other."
—Burton Hillis

Word Ladder (page 55)

Answers may vary. COAL, coat, boat, boas, boys, TOYS

174

Christmas Wordplay (page 55)

The missing word is BANANA. The third and fourth letters of the five words, reading down, would then be SANTA CLAUS.

Webword (page 56)

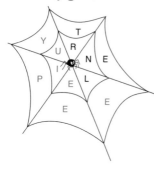

Toy Heaven (page 56)

Santa's workshop

Word Columns (page 57)

There is a remarkable breakdown of taste and intelligence during the holidays. Mature, responsible grownups wear lampshades and drink beverages with raw egg yolks in them.

Word Jigsaw (page 58)

Christmas Acrostic (page 60)

A. hearth; B. chauffeurs; C. front teeth; D. meteorites; E. grandparents; F. toupees; G. whips; H. choirs; I. frostiest

"What is Christmas? It is tenderness for the past, courage for the present, hope for the future."

Webword (page 61)

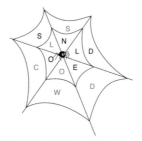

Say What? (page 61)

"Christmas is love in action. Every time we love, every time we give, it's Christmas."

Gingerbread House (page 62)

The leftover letters spell: "Other possible words include genius, horrid, reason, serene, and dashing."

Christmas Tunes (page 64)

G	L	A	M		S	C	U	D		S	I	M	B	A
R	A	N	I		T	U	B	E		E	T	O	Y	S
E	S	T	S		U	S	E	S		N	E	N	E	H
W	H	I	T	E	C	H	R	I	S	T	M	A	S	
		L	A	C	Y			H	R	S				
L	I	K	E	S	O		A	R	I	A		T	R	U
U	N	I	T	E		A	L	A	N		R	A	I	N
C	A	R	O	L	O	F	T	H	E	B	E	L	L	S
E	L	B	E		U	T	E	S		E	V	O	K	E
S	L	Y		C	Z	A	R		E	V	E	N	E	R
		A	Y	E		D	U	E	L					
	J	I	N	G	L	E	B	E	L	L	R	O	C	K
R	O	D	I	N		R	O	T	O		I	S	O	N
M	E	E	S	E		R	O	E	G		E	L	L	E
S	L	E	E	T		S	P	R	Y		S	O	M	E

Christmas Message (page 66)

A. sugar cookies; B. Noah;
C. Drummer Boy; D. stunt;
E. peace on Earth; F. revelers;
G. buffet; H. thrifty; I. unite;
J. tipsy

"Open your presents at Christmastime but be thankful year round for the gifts you receive."

Name Calling (page 67)

"Christmas isn't a season, it's a feeling."

Word Ladder (page 68)

Answers may vary. SLED, sued, sues, hues, hugs, huge, LUGE

How Big a Tree? (page 68)

"Never worry about the size of your Christmas tree. In the eyes of children, they are all 30 feet tall."

—Larry Wilde, "The Merry Book of Christmas"

Christmas Favorite (page 69)

The leftover letters spell: "Poem by Clement Clarke Moore."

On the Tree (page 70)

Word Jigsaw (page 72)

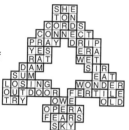

Christmas Acrostic (page 74)

A. photos; B. unity; C. hatching; D. unfortunate; E. sleigh ride; F. joyous; G. sabotages; H. monographs

"One good thing about Christmas shopping—it toughens you for January sales.

Word Columns (page 75)

Many banks have a new kind of Christmas club in operation. The new club helps you save money to pay for last year's gifts.

"The ____ before Christmas" (page 76)

D	E	C	A	L		G	E	R	M		D	A	I	S
I	L	O	V	E		R	U	B	E		Y	M	C	A
M	Y	W	O	N	D	E	R	I	N	G	E	Y	E	S
			C	O	A	T		A	O	R	T	A	S	
R	I	C	A		W	E	B	B		U	S	A	G	E
E	M	O	T	E		L	A	U	E	R		N	E	D
M	A	N	I	L	A		L	L	A	M	A			
		J	O	L	L	Y	O	L	D	E	L	F		
			N	I	K	O	N		S	T	O	O	G	E
S	C	H		P	A	G	E	S		S	N	O	R	E
T	O	A	S	T		A	Y	E	S		G	L	E	N
E	N	T	A	I	L			A	A	A	S			
P	R	A	N	C	E	R	A	N	D	V	I	X	E	N
P	A	R	T		T	A	L	C		E	D	I	T	H
E	D	I	E		O	G	L	E		R	E	V	E	L

Christmas Morning (page 78)

1. Time different on clock; 2. new card on the mantel; 3. book missing—perhaps "A Christmas Carol" to read later?; 4. star turned; 5. mug is larger (Dad needed more coffee); 6. pocket missing from Mom's robe; 7. girl's ponytail grew; 8. gingerbread man on tree ran away; 9. coffee table design altered; 10. window added to boy's package; 11. wrapping paper design changed to snowmen; 12. bow disappeared.

Acrostic (page 80)

A. mishaps; B. Passion; C. charities; D. jittery; E. turtledoves; F. pilaf; G. myrrh; H. whiteout; I. scarves; J. audio

"Christmas is not just a day. . . It is a spirit which should permeate every part of our lives."

The First Christmas (page 81)

1	2	3	4	5	6	7	8	9	10	11	12	13
C	X	I	T		M	A	R	Y	N	D	V	F	Q

14	15	16	17	18	19	20	21	22	23	24	25	26
G	L	W		J	O	S	E	P	H	U	K	Z	B

Word Columns (page 82)

The mark of a good action is that it appears inevitable in retrospect.

Word Ladder (page 83)

Answers may vary. GIFT, rift, riot, root, boot, boat, brat, bray, tray, trap, WRAP

Word Jigsaw (page 84)

Santa's Grotto (page 86)

1. Snowing only in one spot; 2. sleigh has no reindeer; 3. Easter egg present; 4. ice cream truck in winter; 5. man has antlers; 6. torches on ice cream truck; 7. grotto sign pointing the wrong way; 8. pig in line; 9. girl in swimsuit and flippers; 10. guy sitting upside down on bench; 11. "always walk" sign; 12. giant footprint; 13. merry spelled "marry"; 14. cat in tree; 15. snowman has banana nose; 16. apostrophes missing from Santa's Grotto signs; 17. man's pant legs two different colors.

Tasty Scramblegram (page 87)

Well-Loved Carols (page 88)

Word Ladder (page 90)

Answers may vary. SING, sins, tins, tons, toes, noes, NOEL

Sound of Silence? (page 90)

Love is what's in the room with you at Christmas if you stop opening presents and listen.
—Author unknown

Let It Shine (page 91)

Presents for Kids (page 92)

The leftover letters spell: "Nothing is as mean as giving a child something useful for Christmas."

Christmas Songs (page 94)

Christmas Tree (page 98)

Leftover letters spell: "The best Yuletide decoration is to be wreathed in a smile."

Word Jigsaw (page 96)

Food for Thought (page 100)

Say What? (page 102)

"When we recall Christmas past, we usually find that the simplest things—not the great occasions—give off the greatest glow of happiness."

Noel (page 102)

```
L O E N N O L O
O O N O L O L N
E N O N O N E E
L E N O E E O N
N O L O N O O L
O L N O E N N L
L E O L E L E O
E N E L O L E N
```

Stargazer (page 103)

Group I: stars 2, 7, 11, and 15; Group II: stars 3, 5, and 12; Group III: stars 4, 9, and 14; Group IV: stars 1 and 13; Group V: stars 6 and 10; Group VI: star 8.

Christmas at the Movies (page 104)

Picture This (page 106)

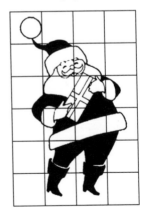

Singer's Dream (page 106)

"Unless we make Christmas an occasion to share our blessings, all the snow in Alaska won't make it 'white.'"
—Bing Crosby

Ornament (page 110)

Ornaments (Part II) (page 108)

Santa, elf, snowman, reindeer, sleigh bell

What's in a Name? Ask Santa (page 112)

Word-a-Maze: Iced Orbs (page 109)

Word Columns (page 114)

I stopped believing in Santa Claus when my mother took me to see him in a department store and he asked for my autograph.

ANSWER KEY

Santa (page 115)

```
A N S A T N A N T S
T A A S A N N T T A
N S N A A A N T A S
A A N A S T S A N T
N N N A N S A T S T N
S A T T A N T A N T
S T S A A S N N T A
A A N S A T S N S T
T N T A T A A T N A
A S A N A S N A A S
```

Picture This (page 118)

Riddle (page 115)

New Year's Day is always 7 days after Christmas Day. Therefore, they both land on the same day of the week. However, New Year's Day and Christmas Day of the same year can never be on the same day of the week.

Decorations (page 118)

ornamentation

Word Columns (page 119)

It's snowing still," said Eeyore gloomily. "So it is." "And freezing." "Is it?" "Yes," said Eeyore. "However," he said, brightening up a little, "we haven't had an earthquake lately."
—A. A. Milne

Deck the Halls (page 116)

Snowflake (page 120)

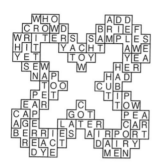

Picture This (page 122)

Word Ladder (page 123)

Answers may vary. STAR, stay, slay, play, pray, tray, trey, TREE

Christmas Mix-Up (page 123)

1. "The Nutcracker";
2. "Silent Night"; 3. "The Gift of the Magi"; 4. "It's a Wonderful Life"

Colorful Scramblegram (page 124)

Word Ladder (page 125)

Answers may vary. SNOW, show, chow, chop, coop, coos, cops, CAPS

The Three Kings (page 125)

Christmas Crossword (page 126)

A	N	D		R	O	T		C	A	R	E	S
B	O	O		A	R	E		A	D	U	L	T
S	N	O	W	M	A	N		M	O	M	M	Y
E	R	R		T	O	N	E	R				
		O	P	E	R	A		E	A	S	T	
N	A	N	A		S	P	A		C	O	O	
J	I	N	G	L	E		S	I	L	E	N	T
A	N	T		S	A	T		D	A	D	S	
B	E	E	T		R	I	T	E	S			
		O	W	N	E	R		S	E	A		
W	H	I	T	E		R	U	D	O	L	P	H
A	I	R	E	D		E	C	O		L	E	E
S	T	E	M	S		D	E	N		A	D	S

Christmas Tree (page 128)

Silent Night (page 130)

1. fireplace piece missing;
2. stocking disappeared;
3. candle burned out; 4. cherry removed from cake; 5. pony's leg vanished; 6. robot's stripes filled in; 7. doll's blush rubbed off; 8. car piece missing;
9. dollhouse lamp vanished;
10. dollhouse tub gone; 11. it stopped snowing; 12. robot's claw missing; 13. ornament disappeared; 14. candy cane eaten; 15. dollhouse chimney blew its top; 16. robot's mouth shorter

Trees & Stars (page 132)

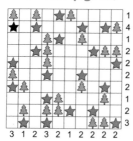

Acrostic (page 133)

A. sermon; B. misanthrope;
C. inhibit; D. wintertime;
E. clench; F. toasts; G. shahs;
H. holidays; I. thrash

"The only blind person at Christmastime is he who has not Christmas in his heart."

Star of David (page 134)

Winter Wonders and Woes (page 136)

Words Found in "Christmas" (page 138)

Say What? (page 140)

"No matter how carefully you stored the lights last year, they will be snarled again this Christmas."

Addagram (page 140)

The missing letter is R.

Pearl, silver, emerald, crystal

What's the Missing Word? (page 141)

1. teeth; 2. deck; 3. frosty; 4. grandma; 5. merry; 6. mommy; 7. home; 8. bells; 9. rock; 10. snow; 11. red-nosed; 12. drummer; 13. wonderland; 14. twelve; 15. white

Food (page 142)

O	A	F	S		D	E	E	R		M	O	M
F	I	L	M		I	S	L	E		I	D	A
F	R	U	I	T	C	A	K	E		N	O	R
			R	O	E			D	E	C	R	Y
S	A	C	K	S		T	H	Y	M	E		
N	T	H		C	A	R	D		S	P	A	S
O	R	E		A	B	E	T	S		I	C	E
W	A	S	H		L	E	V	I		E	N	E
	T	A	M	E	S		L	A	S	E	R	
S	A	N	T	A		A	L	S				
L	O	U		C	A	N	D	Y	C	A	N	E
A	N	T		A	L	O	E		O	P	A	L
Y	E	S		W	E	T	S		T	E	T	S

Christmas Time (page 144)

Word Columns (page 146)

"Blessed is the season which engages the whole world in a conspiracy of love."

Say What? (page 150)

"I once bought my kids a set of batteries for Christmas with a note on it saying, 'toys not included.'"

Christmas Presents (page 147)

1	2	3	4	5	6	7	8	9	10	11	12	13
E	U	C	W	G	I	F	T	S	H	O	P	N
14	15	16	17	18	19	20	21	22	23	24	25	26
Z	L	Q	K	V	J	Y	M	X	A	B	R	D

Decorating the Tree (page 148)

The leftover letters spell: "Saint Boniface is credited with the invention of the Christmas tree."

Age-Old Question (page 150)

My birthday is December 31. The day I made the statement was January 1. So, 2 days ago (December 30) I was 18, and on December 31, I turned 19; I will be 20 on December 31 of this year, and next year on December 31, I will be 21.

Window Shopping (page 151)

1. the awning fringe; 2. record for a wreath; 3. tinsel is not complete; 4. tinsel hanging outside window frame; 5. snowman's hat on upside down; 6. Easter egg on tree; 7. paper boat hat on toy Santa; 8. boy in window has one mitten; 9. boy has one short sleeve; 10. floating head on right; 11. man dressed for summer; 12. woman holding child has basketball for hat; 13. rope going through kid's jacket collar; 14. mom's collar different on one side; 15. girl has only one earmuff; 16. hat and coat with no person.

Word Columns (page 152)

"Did you ever notice that life seems to follow certain patterns? Like I noticed that every year around this time, I hear Christmas music."

Decorations (Part II) (page 154)

stocking, garland, ornaments, angel, lights, tree

Webword (page 155)

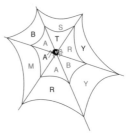

Say What? (page 155)

"Christmas is doing a little something extra for someone."

Name Calling (page 156)

"Christmas is love in action."

Magic Tree (page 157)

What Can You Fit in a Christmas Stocking? (page 158)

1. king; 2. ink; 3. coins; 4. stink; 5. knot; 6. stock; 7. sign; 8. sing; 9. skin; 10. tick

Holiday Wordplay (page 158)

The letters A C E H I M R S T Y can be rearranged to spell CHEMISTRY: A.

Word Columns (page 159)

Once again, we come to the holiday season, a deeply religious time that each of us observes, in his own way, by going to the mall of his choice.

Santa's Helpers (page 160)

B	E	A	S	T		D	E	W		B	I	B
A	L	I	T	O		E	L	I		U	T	E
A	L	L	E	N		N	I	E	L	S	E	N
		T	Y	P	E	S		A	T	M		
A	M	C		A	B	H	O	R				
L	E	A	D	O	N		A	R	I	E	L	
A	S	N	E	R			C	A	B	O	T	
	H	A	M	E	L		Q	A	T	A	R	I
	A	S	I	D	E			N	I	X		
U	R	N		V	I	D	A	L				
B	R	I	D	G	E	S		H	A	N	K	S
R	A	N		A	R	C		E	L	I	O	T
O	L	D		B	Y	O		M	A	N	D	Y

Oh Christmas Tree (page 164)

Holiday Puzzler (page 162)

Charles Dickens, Christmas carols, Saint Nick, Tiny Tim, poinsettia plant. The missing letters spell SANTA.

Merry Scrambled Christmas! (page 162)

1. Christmas tree; 2. three wise men; 3. nativity scene

Festive Fare (page 163)

1	2	3	4	5	6	7	8	9	10	11	12	13
H	D	O	V	L	Z	F	S	N	W	A	I	Q

14	15	16	17	18	19	20	21	22	23	24	25	26
C	P	X	T	U	R	K	E	Y	J	G	M	B